SIMPLE
ORGA

LY
ANIC

A COOKBOOK FOR SUSTAINABLE, SEASONAL, AND LOCAL INGREDIENTS

BY JESSE ZIFF COOL

PHOTOGRAPHS BY FRANCE RUFFENACH

CHRONICLE BOOKS

SAN FRANCISCO

First Chronicle Books LLC edition published in 2008

Text copyright © 2000 and 2008 by Jesse Ziff Cool.
Photographs copyright © 2008 by France Ruffenach.
All rights reserved. No part of this book may be
reproduced in any form without written permission
from the publisher.

Library of Congress Cataloging-in-Publication
Data available.

ISBN: 978-0-8118-6044-4

Manufactured in China.

Prop styling by Sara Slavin
Food styling by Karen Shinto
Designed by Sara Schneider
Typesetting by Janis Reed

10 9 8 7 6 5 4 3 2 1

Chronicle Books LLC
680 Second Street
San Francisco, California 94107

www.chroniclebooks.com

DEDICATION

To my farmer friends, the tireless workers of the land who grow our food and continue to teach me and every good cook the real definition of gourmet food.

To my father, who grew organic food in our backyard, enjoyed cooking for and feeding others, and sparked my lust for flavor.

To my mother, who gave me the insight that nurturing and love belong on every plate and must find a place at every meal, at every table.

For my sons, Joshua and Jonah, who lived through the wonderful turmoil of the ever-changing politics of organic and sustainable cuisine. As unfashionable as it might have seemed at the time, they found themselves growing gardens, working on pig farms, and cooking for themselves, their families, and loved ones. They now know that food is not only for sustenance, but is also for creating joy and happiness for oneself and others.

ACKNOWLEDGMENTS

Amy Treadwell and Bill LeBlond, at Chronicle Books, realized that the first edition of this book just might have been ahead of its time. Thank you for resurrecting *Your Organic Kitchen*. I truly enjoy working with you.

I had no idea how to breathe new life into *YOK*, which remains my favorite of all of my books. It took some searching, but I found my dear friend and the original editor, Anne Egan. Together, and I mean *together*, we combed through information and researched and assembled what we considered a sensible and practical book about organic and sustainable food. Anne, also passionate about organics, has always enjoyed my recipes (a cook's dream come true), and I continue to deeply appreciate working with her. Thank you, Anne! Deborah Kops, thank you for your thorough copyediting job.

All of the companies, organizations, farmers, ranchers, fishermen, dairymen, bakers, and cooks who have made my life richer and taught me about the basic goodness in choosing healthy options (most of the time!), I thank you.

And finally, my earnest gratitude goes to my entire staff at CoolEatz Restaurants and Catering. They are the gatekeepers who watch and care and work daily on the path of walking the walk and staying true to our beliefs. It is not easy in this ever-changing arena of natural foods. The restaurant business is almost as thankless and volatile as farming. To attempt to do it with kindness, safety, and love is important. It ain't perfect, and each time we falter, we get right back up and work to get better and learn more. From the person who cleans the dishes to the one who serves the food, we know, honor, and appreciate how important each of you is to our simple organic kitchen.

CONTENTS

INTRODUCTION

I was a fortunate kid. My family's riches weren't measured in dollars but in the love that we felt and, in many ways, in the healthy foods that we ate. For the most part, our food was free of artificial flavors, preservatives, chemicals, and pesticides. My family wasn't on a deliberate organic crusade. We simply respected the old traditional ways of growing, gathering, and preparing foods in the healthiest and cleanest manner possible.

This philosophy of respecting and revering food goes back generations in my family—on both sides. I was blessed to have Jewish and Italian grandparents who loved to garden and cook. As a little girl growing up in a rural town near Pittsburgh, I remember helping my parents and grandparents tend their small backyard gardens. They taught me about living heirlooms—treasured seeds brought from the Old Country that they respectfully planted in American soil. They raised their own chickens, and my uncle Jack owned a slaughterhouse where naturally grazed cattle were processed and aged properly.

Cooking and sharing food at the dinner table were always at the heart of our household. Being Jewish and Italian meant endless conversations about both food and life itself. Because of this rich ethnic mix, our months were filled with celebrations that featured tables loaded with delicious dishes, and homes full of laughing, loving family and friends. Bottles of cooking wine and olive oil were always present. Plates were always piled with greens, both fresh and steamed. Garlic was as common a seasoning as salt and pepper. Onions seemed to find their way into nearly every dish.

My grandmother Edna was a remarkable cook. She taught me how to make ravioli and other dishes from scratch. She got the meat from Uncle Jack, roasted it, and cooked it for what seemed like an eternity. While the meat slowly simmered, she went to work making homemade pasta. My two brothers would be outside playing, while I would happily be by Nana's side in the kitchen, learning how to make ravioli, polenta, and platters full of slow-cooked meats and vegetables. This was my idea of playtime well spent. I can almost smell the inviting aromas of those memories. To this day, cooking and eating good food are among the deepest pleasures of my life.

I still chuckle recalling all those times when Papa, my Italian grandfather, cajoled me into accompanying him on his "special missions" to pluck wild dandelions and onions from yards all over the neighborhood. We would rush home, rinse the leaves, season them with a little olive oil, salt, and pepper, and enjoy our green treat.

My parents, Eddie and June, continued this organic-food tradition. My mom was the family nurturer, always there with soft, gentle hugs. To this day she has believed in me and encouraged me to pursue my dreams and refuse to sacrifice my integrity as an owner of organic and sustainable restaurants. When my dad passed away, he was actually at the Menlo Park Farmers' Market, where he was still selling produce for our dear farmer friend, Stuart Dickson. Dad never retired. He just kept peddling food, as he had done his entire life. For thirteen years, he was a revered member of the community, showing up every Saturday and Sunday, rain or shine, to meet and greet his fans and share tips on how to cook or eat whatever Stuart packed in the truck.

I couldn't have asked for a more perfect start on this journey. Gardening with my dad as he instilled in me his passion and joy in watching something grow, and later paying homage to the fruits of our labor at the table, were the best lessons for an organic-minded cook. I remember those early Saturday mornings when as a young girl, I heard the sounds of a truck pulling into our driveway with yet another load of organic material for our garden. Dad relied on natural remedies to solve pest problems without resorting to pesticides and was rewarded with the neighborhood's juiciest and biggest tomatoes. His garden stretched everywhere in the yard, including between the shrubbery, where he planted melons and cucumbers.

THE AGELESS VALUE OF FOOD

Natural food remedies were a part of my family's medicine chest. Garlic and onions were used as herbal medicines to fight off colds and fevers, in addition to flavoring our cooking. I was taught that eating the right foods keeps you healthy. It's just that simple. I believe in that. Most of us in the family don't take vitamins. We don't see the need. We get all our nutrients from a well-balanced diet that includes lots of organic foods that we eat daily.

The way my parents ate and spent their lives together was living proof of the benefits of following this philosophy. I associate their

sixty-two years of passionate marriage with the wholesome food that they always ate—that, and their lasting love for each other. This healthy lifestyle explains my mother's youthful attitude today. Even though she is now in her late eighties, she is still full of spunk.

THE ORGANIC FAMILY TRADITION CONTINUES

Decades have passed since my childhood. Now, I am a mother of two sons, and I have two grandchildren. Just like my grandparents and parents, I too am passing on the family tradition of supporting organic gardening and cooking.

It hasn't been easy convincing my sons at times. My older son, Joshua, still jokes about what it was like to have a mom who was a hippie. At school, no one would trade lunches with him. Joshua complained that, compared with the processed foods of his peers, his lunches tasted like dry canned food on sandpaper bread. He grew up before good-tasting organic products were readily available.

At school barbecues, Joshua was the only student stepping up to the grill with tofu and veggie hot dogs. He grew up thinking that crackers were cookies—until he got to school and learned the truth. Later, as most teens tend to do, he rebelled and turned into a junk-food junkie. He nicknamed me Granola Head and Earth Hugger.

Now that they are parents, Joshua and his wife, Yuko, understand why I insisted on feeding my children organic foods. It was done out of love and concern for their health. Determined to keep their son, Masa, and daughter, Miya, healthy, Joshua and Yuko are careful about the foods they provide. They grow a garden and cook from scratch. They make sure to sit down for a family meal nearly every evening. And the kids eat a wide variety of food—broccoli, spinach, carrots, avocado, mango, mussels, clams, dishes with herbs and spices—because that is what they have been offered from the very beginning.

Jonah, my younger son, embraced the organic philosophy more easily. I occasionally let him "junk out" on processed foods, while trying to gently enlighten him about the benefits of fresh foods. Now a young adult, Jonah prefers to eat organic and locally grown foods and makes very wise choices.

When Jonah was in high school, our kitchen was known among his buddies as the place for the best-tasting after-school snacks. The refrigerator was often filled with homemade pastas, soups, and healthy munchies. No artificial ingredients or chemicals were in any of the foods that I prepared. Beyond organic, this was and remains my bottom-line philosophy: Food is just food, and stay away from additives and GMO foods whenever possible.

Now Jonah is working on a Ph.D. in cellular biology at Duke University. Through farmer friends, we found a local organic farm near Durham, North Carolina, where Jonah volunteers during his spare time. Cane Creek Farm is owned by an awesome farm woman, Eliza McClean, who raises animals and produce, which she sells at the Saturday market. Jonah regularly feeds the pigs, goats, and chickens; mends fences; and gathers eggs. While dedicated to his lab work, he manages to maintain a connection to locally produced food and the people who grow it. He loves to cook for himself and others, knowing that, in the midst of the serious work he is doing, this brings joy to himself and others. I am not sure whether I am more proud of his accomplishments in science or in the barnyard, including the morning he discovered and had to tend to a dozen brand-new piglets in the barn.

When I was asked once what legacy, if any, I wanted to leave behind, I replied: That my children will, under any circumstance, know how to plant seeds, to grow food. That they too will find satisfaction in cooking for themselves and others. That they will feel nourished when they open a refrigerator to leftovers from the food they prepared from scratch!

They can still look out the back door of my house and see a garden. But now they are no longer embarrassed because of my chickens, clucking about in the middle of suburban Palo Alto, California. My family now appreciates what it means to taste healthy, real eggs from chickens that are fed organically. My grandchildren love to come to "Mima's" house and go to the garden to gather whatever is in season, including eggs. Then they pull up a stool and cook by my side.

I share these stories as a parent to let you know how important it is to practice what you believe, and trust that, in time, your children will see the love and commitment behind your decision to eat organic foods whenever given the choice. At the same time, I accept that my children and I are a part of the real world. We need to do our best to live honorably and respectfully on the planet.

My goal as a parent and now a grandparent has always been just to make my family conscious of what they eat. Even in the midst of their busy and hectic lives, I want them to maintain that vision of me standing at the prep table cooking with love for them. And, from what I can see, as they become adults, they are doing exactly the same for their loved ones.

A LIFELONG LOVE OF COOKING

By now, it's easy to see how I view myself: After all these years of cooking at home and in my restaurants, the title of chef does not sit well and seems overused. We are all simply cooks, and I am a very contented one. Feeding others makes me happy. So does being treated to a special meal prepared by a loved one. Naturally, I prefer the ingredients to be organic, but I take more joy in knowing that someone has taken the time to cook for me. The spirit in which a dish is prepared is often as nurturing as the food itself.

I grew up during the 1950s, a decade characterized by the emergence of processed foods. Even my family was seduced at times by the allure of fast foods and convenience foods. A lunchtime sandwich often consisted of a freshly picked organic tomato and a handful of lettuce from my dad's garden between two slices of Wonder Bread, slathered with Miracle Whip.

This explains my realistic view of organics. I am conscious of and careful about what I eat. Although there are times when there is nothing better than a corned beef and chopped liver sandwich at a Jewish deli, my pantry is predominantly organic and free of artificial ingredients and chemicals. My restaurants feature organic ingredients on the menus, but we are even more committed to using locally grown and produced ingredients, which may not be organic. I walk the walk, but I am not ashamed to occasionally wander off the path. I like to follow what I call the 80/20 rule. My kids subscribe to this, and it is a welcome part of what I share with others. For 80 to 85 percent of the time, be a zealot. Eat healthy, clean, organic, and safe foods. Exercise and be conscious and conscientious about caring for your body, food, and environment.

For the other 15 to 20 percent of the time, live in the real world and choose your poisons well. We are human beings, and since the beginning of time, humans have chosen to eat and do things that are not always healthy. It is part of being a real person in the real world. So, for this small percentage of time, go for it—eat, drink, and be merry, but do it with awareness. And make sure that most of the time, you are taking good care of yourself, your family, and loved ones.

GIVING BACK TO THE COMMUNITY

I give credit to my parents for my business success. Each of them contributed in different ways.

During my childhood, Dad reigned as King Eddie, owner of King Edward's Supermarket in Greensburg, Pennsylvania. He ran his store with integrity and respect for his customers and employees. He would wow customers with his array of locally grown meats and produce, which were most often naturally organic. He ran a German-style bakery; the bakers never used prepared mixes, and made fruit pies, whole grain breads, and even doughnuts from scratch. My dad delighted in creating custard from whole milk and churning gallons of strawberry and peach ice cream made with fresh fruit, again usually organic, grown on local farms. By age twelve, in order to be near my hard-working father, I was working side by side with him and loving every minute.

My dad taught me what it meant to be a part of the community. He often organized benefits to help those in need. And so even during lean times in my first restaurant, when the staff would urge me to cut back on costs, we tried to maintain a level of charity and civic work.

At the age of twenty-seven, I opened my first organic restaurant with my first husband, Bob, and a buddy of his, Steve Silva. We used as many organic ingredients as we could find. At that time, there were no organic restaurants, so buying enough organic ingredients was challenging. Still, we were determined to serve food that was healthy for people and the environment. After a long search, we finally found a local produce company that delivered organic fruits and vegetables. It was called the 3:30 A.M. Produce Company, and it was run by two wonderful, dynamic, high-spirited women, Cathi Lerch and Patricia Atkins. In those early years, we would also hit the farmers' market every Saturday to buy produce. It was the only option for buying local, organic ingredients. We had Muir Glen tomatoes (which were organic) delivered by UPS and searched endlessly for other foods that were not tainted with anything artificial. In the early '70s, this was not an easy task.

We were told over and over again that using organic and sustainably produced ingredients in a restaurant wasn't realistic from a cost perspective. There were times when things got tough, and it was my mother who supported my bottom line: The use of organic products was more important than making lots of money. Now, after more than thirty years in the restaurant business, I feel incredibly successful. One of the keys to this success has been the use of as much organic food as possible while serving a seasonal menu. Seasonal fresh foods always tend to be less expensive, and the flavors are deep and genuine. The somewhat trendy concept of using local, seasonal, and organic ingredients was not cutting-edge back then. Only a handful of people understood that we were not only serving delicious food, but also felt responsible for their health and safety.

Bob and Steve moved on to other arenas, but I kept on the sustainable path in the restaurant business. I feel great gratitude for what we did together back in those early days.

Every day, in fact, I feel profoundly grateful to everyone who has been patient and supportive of my efforts—my family, my staff, and my customers. As you can see, food was and remains my heart and soul. As a daughter, a mother, a grandmother, and a business owner, I maintain my unwavering commitment to using organic foods as often as possible. To me, restaurants as well as home kitchens should be places where food is simply as pure as it can be, and is always served with love.

WHY ORGANIC?

Let's consider what our great-grandparents grew up eating. Most likely, they enjoyed vine-ripened tomatoes and juicy red strawberries grown in nutrient-rich soil, pampered with fresh spring water, and warmed by sunshine. The fruits and vegetables were probably grown by a local farmer whom everyone knew by his first name. In this kind of community food system, there is a face attached to the production of the food people eat.

Our ancestors grew up in a time when "fresh," "natural," and "organic" went without saying, and there was no need to give food special labels. The primary food additives were natural preservatives and seasonings like vinegar and salt, and not difficult-to-pronounce, strange-sounding chemicals like monosodium glutamate and sodium nitrate. Our great-grandmothers planned their meals around foods of the season, and during the long winters they relied on the local produce they had canned and preserved the previous summer and autumn, which was better than fresh food shipped from afar, just as preserved local food is usually preferable today.

The fruits and vegetables they ate were naturally grown, unadulterated organic foods. But the term "organic" was never mentioned. For them, food was fresh, celebrated as the seasons came and went, and, most of all, safe for them and their loved ones.

These days most supermarket tomatoes spend their infancy inside huge greenhouses. They are nursed with synthetic fertilizers and engineered for shelf life and visual appeal, rather than flavor. After their stay in the greenhouse, they are transplanted to mile-wide fields saturated with 400 to 600 pounds per acre of more fertilizer and are fumigated with methyl bromide, a weed-killing toxic gas. Weekly, crop planes unleash fungicides and insecticides that destroy plant pests and diseases—and, unfortunately, some migrating birds. But the public has been led to believe that these are the best kind of tomatoes because they are inexpensive, uniform, and perfect-looking.

Many of us health-conscious eaters, however, desire and even demand that foods from supermarkets and restaurants be as good and pure as foods enjoyed by families who lived three generations ago. Our voices were stifled for a few decades, but as public awareness has evolved, we are being heard and respected. Finally, "you are what you eat" is no longer being discounted.

Look around you. Signs of this retro food revolution are everywhere. Even as recently as the 1980s, supermarkets separated tomatoes strictly by type—plum or beefsteak, for instance. Now, they are distinguished by variety, color, and how they are grown.

In many stores, there are now more choices. Look for the smaller tomato section, the one that is vibrant with a vast array of colors and shapes, and, yes, the tomatoes that typically cost a little more per pound. There is a good chance that you will spot the Certified Organic label—a signal to health-conscious shoppers that each and every one of these red, gold, purple, and green beauties enjoyed a splendid beginning. They developed from seeds that inherently have unique flavors, have not been genetically modified, and were grown in nutrient-rich soil on small, local organic farms free of artificial chemicals, pesticides, and commercial fertilizers.

This return to organic vegetables extends beyond your local supermarket. Many restaurant owners now proudly highlight their menus with organically prepared dishes, showcasing the farms' names and indicating their preference for organically raised foods.

THE HISTORY OF ORGANIC FARMING

Who should we thank for starting the organic food movement? Perhaps the better question is, who rescued it and brought it back? Before 1900, all food was organically grown. Of course, farmers and shoppers didn't call it by that phrase. They didn't need to. They knew that what they ate came from a local farmer who had grown the food with care, love, and purity. There was no reason to be concerned about safety or pollution.

Then the age of mass production arrived, intermingled with a couple of world wars. America had many more mouths to feed. We needed to grow lots of food in a hurry. Scientists discovered that chemicals sprayed on crops could kill pests and plant diseases instantly. They also developed artificial flavorings to perk up people's palates, and preservatives to make foods last longer and maintain an eye-catching appearance. Growers in south Florida began loading their produce onto large trucks and train cars, to be delivered to supermarkets all over the country, as far as 3,000 miles away.

A few visionaries began questioning the price that our bodies and our planet were paying for this technology, born of our haste to produce foods more quickly. Sir Albert Howard, a British agricultural scientist, was the first to consciously reject modern "agri-chemical" methods back in the 1930s. He argued that artificial fertilizers and poisonous insecticides had no place in farming. He figured out a way to turn town wastes—animal manure, compost, grass turf, and straw—into usable nutrient materials, which were tilled into the soil to nourish plants in a safe way. He called this nutrient recycling system the Wheel of Life.

Here in the United States, J. I. Rodale embraced Sir Albert's views. It was Rodale who in 1940 popularized the term "organic." Rodale had left New York City and purchased a sixty-five-acre farm in rural eastern Pennsylvania. He grew all his crops without chemical fertilizers or pesticides. Rodale strongly believed that healthy soil produces healthy foods, which in turn help keep people healthy. He began sharing his philosophy in 1942, when he founded *Organic Gardening* magazine, a publication now run by his grandchildren. He remains one of my first heroes in the organic farming movement.

Even back in the 1940s, Rodale warned that using pesticides and artificial fertilizers would pollute our farmlands, lakes, rivers, and air. An excerpt from his book *Pay Dirt* (1945) reads: "People felt they could afford—with a continent to develop—to wear out a farm and move to another. That day has passed. Badly eroded, worn-out soil will not recover overnight, but fertility can be restored. Land still fertile can be kept so, with composts, and be constantly improved."

There are many modern-day heroes carrying forth these beliefs. They range from the founders of organic food companies to the small local farmers doing their bit, one acre at a time. Behind the scenes are researchers studying the health advantages of organic foods and many nonprofit organizations supporting the environment and sustainable politics. I salute all those working for this great cause.

HEALTH REASONS TO CHOOSE ORGANIC

Remember all those times your mom said, "Drink your milk!" and "Eat your fruits and vegetables. They're good for you!"? Many of us growing up in the '50s, '60s, and '70s scoffed at those messages. Hamburgers, french fries, and chocolate malts tasted so much better.

But Mom was right. Nutritionists and doctors, backed by scientific evidence, continue telling us that fresh fruits and vegetables are loaded with essential vitamins and minerals, which we need to keep our bodies healthy. Doesn't it make sense that the foods we eat and the nutrients they contain would affect the functioning of our bodies? We now know that blueberries, for instance, contain antioxidants, known to fight off cancer-causing free radical molecules. Broccoli and milk are loaded with calcium, which we need to maintain strong bones. And this is just the beginning.

Rather than just hearing that real food is good for us, we are learning how and why it is life-supportive. I remember when I was invited to speak about organic cooking to physicians and medical students at Stanford University School of Medicine a few years back. After serving them a luscious and beautiful lunch made with all organic ingredients, I asked them how they felt. Many responded with one word:

"Great!" I then asked them to think of their bodies as they might their cars. "Many of you will someday drive an expensive car," I said, "and I doubt if you would even consider putting cheap fuel into the tanks of your cars. Think, then, of food as our fuel. Eat the best foods, and your body will run smoothly."

Throughout the 1990s, the healthy-eating campaign nudged us a little toward eating better, but what really brought it to the forefront was the issue of food safety. Remember the milk scare in the 1990s? Is it any wonder that many people, even those who are not committed to the organic food movement, still avoid cow's milk? The public responded to the fact that some commercial farmers were injecting their cows with a genetically engineered hormone called recombinant bovine growth hormone (rBGH). Some researchers saw a possible link between rBGH and certain cancers, such as breast and prostate.

While most conventional dairy farmers continue to use these hormones today, organic farmers never give their cows growth hormones or antibiotics. All their milk, cheese, and other dairy products are free from these substances. The cows are given a wholesome diet of organic grains and feed. Better yet, if you can find raw milk products from a reliable dairy, that's your very best option because many people seem to find it easier to digest.

Of the many issues that are connected with food safety, the presence of pesticides in the foods we eat is a big concern. Large amounts have been found in what would otherwise be considered wholesome foods. Unfortunately, if you eat out-of-season foods that are not grown organically, and are shipped from all corners of the planet, there is a good chance they are tainted with ripening agents and pesticides.

During winter months, it is not unusual to see New Zealand strawberries, Mexican tomatoes, or Chilean grapes in supermarkets. Researchers at the Rodale Institute in Kutztown, Pennsylvania, determined that a large portion of the fresh food that we eat daily travels an average of 1,400 miles from the farm to our plates. These "food miles" come at a cost to our health. Nonorganic Chilean grapes, for instance, represent 90 percent of all winter grapes consumed

by Americans. Yet they rank among the foods contaminated with the most toxic pesticide residues. This scares me. Whether by ship, plane, or truck, the transportation of these products expends fossil fuels known to increase global warming. This is hardly a sustainable act. They are also usually lacking in flavor, as they must be picked early to withstand the long trips. I believe that supporting small local farms is of paramount importance. In general, even when local produce is not Certified Organic, if it has been raised with organic techniques, I actually prefer it to Certified Organic produce that had to travel to get to me.

Eating locally adds another dimension to your meals. To eat locally, you must eat seasonally. In today's supermarkets, most fruits and vegetables are available year-round. They are not grown locally or even nationally year-round, though. So much of this produce is imported. Eating seasonally is about eating the produce that's currently grown in your area.

Of course, if you live in a region where the growing season is short, this is not as easy. But you can find ways to preserve the perfectly ripe and flavorful fruits and vegetables of the warmer months for use during the cold seasons. When we begin to eat seasonally, we become more in touch with our environment and the growing process.

We need fruits, vegetables, and dairy to sustain us and keep our immune systems strong enough to fend off invading viruses and bacteria. So what should we do? In winter, depending upon where you live, opt for plenty of local fresh or organic frozen, canned, and dried fruits and vegetables, especially hearty ones like winter squash and root vegetables. Do not avoid dairy products, meats, or fish. The solution is to be more selective. When given a choice, opt for Certified Organic produce at supermarkets, natural food stores, food cooperatives, farmers' markets, or local farm stands. Buy from and regularly support farmers who you know practice organic cultivation, even if they are not certified. During the winter, eat organic frozen or canned items, especially those from the United States.

There will be times when organic foods are not readily available. When you need to buy conventionally grown fruits and vegetables, make it a habit to thoroughly scrub them under running water to remove traces of chemicals from their skins and crevices. This may make a difference, but if the produce has been grown with soil additives, washing may be a futile attempt to remove anything artificial.

As for dairy products, I choose only organic ones, which are readily available in most supermarkets. To me, it's a safer choice. Others agree. Since the mid-1990s, when rBGH news made headlines, the sale of organic milk has increased by leaps and bounds.

ENVIRONMENTAL REASONS TO CHOOSE ORGANIC

A lot has changed during my time on this planet. Beautiful unspoiled meadows that I remember from the time I was a little girl are paved over with strip malls. Trout-filled streams and lakes now display "off-limits" signs because of pollution. The crystal blue, seemingly invincible sky that I marveled at as a child succumbs a bit more each year to smog and the diminishing ozone layer. As Joni Mitchell sang, "Don't it always seem to go, that you don't know what you've got 'til it's gone? They paved paradise and put up a parking lot."

It's easy to blame vehicle exhaust fumes and industrial waste for the tainting of our land, water, and sky. Yes, they've made an impact. But you may be surprised to learn that agriculture is the biggest polluter. The Environmental Protection Agency has proven that agriculture has polluted one-fourth of all American rivers and streams. American farmers are spraying five times more pesticides than they did in the 1960s.

Each one of us can contribute to cleaning our air, land, and water by making conscious choices each time we shop, prepare meals, and take out the trash. My heroes remain the organic farmers—environmental pioneers who, with commitment and vision, have chosen the old way, opting for compost and other natural fertilizers to create healthy soils that yield healthy plants. Using integrated pest management, they control pests with beneficial insects, not pesticides. They rotate crops to maintain the

soil's fertility. They provide Certified Organic feed to their cows and chickens.

These farmers are doing their part to protect our communities, our soil, water, and air. They recognize the dramatic impact that a single commodity—food—makes on our environment. They are forming alliances and working together for the betterment of all.

I believe that we must support the preservation of farmland, but I hope that someday organic farmers will grow all the food that we eat. In my restaurant, we try to do our part to protect the environment. All of our disposable and to-go packaging can be composted because it is made from plant life. For example, the forks are made from potatoes, the plates from wheat, and the clear cups that look like plastic are actually made from corn. With all the take-out food eaten these days, it is our responsibility to limit our deposits to the mounting landfills.

THE IMPORTANCE OF FLAVOR

I am a cook, a restaurant owner, and a lover of delicious food. I believe that flavor is another important reason to choose organic products. Usually, they have more flavor than their conventional counterparts. This great taste is the reason why many chefs—even those not active in the organic movement—are purchasing organic products. A survey conducted by the National Restaurant Association found that well over 50 percent of restaurants with per-person dinner checks of $25 or more are now offering organic items on their menus.

I suggest that you see for yourself. Taste-test the organic items available on your market's shelves, and you, too, will be a believer. The depth of genuine flavor will convince you that organic products are not only better for you and the environment, but also so much more delicious.

WHY PAY MORE—WILLINGLY?

Cost remains a major issue among newcomers to the organic world. Yes, organic products can cost more in terms of dollars and cents. But you reap the dividends in having a healthier body and knowing that you are promoting sustainable, healthy farms and are not harming the environment. There are still bargains to be found. Locally grown organic foods in season may sometimes cost less than conventionally grown produce shipped over long distances.

Consider these factors, and you will see the true value of buying organic.

1. On organic farms, soil preparation, planting, weed control, and harvesting are often more labor-intensive. Natural pesticides and integrated pest management can be more expensive than pesticides and insecticides. In general, they are far less intrusive to the environment, however.

2. Most organic farmers practice crop rotation, which costs more than planting the same crop season after season in the same location. The advantage of crop rotation is that disease, weed, and insect cycles are interrupted through the rotation process. Nature favors simplicity. The complexity created by rotating crops aids in the control of farm pests.

3. Organic feed for livestock costs more than conventional feed, but you are assured that the livestock are not consuming harmful chemicals that could be passed on to you.

4. Organic crops are frequently harvested at the peak of flavor, so they may have a shorter shelf life.

5. Organic companies often have to spend more money to use recycled paper, plastic, and other materials that decompose in the country's landfills.

SUSTAINABLE CUISINE

The concept of sustainable cuisine embraces the full cycle of what it means to be conscious of how and where our food comes from: how it's grown and produced as well as the people involved in the production.

Many who practice sustainable cuisine use locally produced ingredients and organic foods. They support composting as well as responsible fishing, farming, and meat production. Recycling and using environmentally benign chemicals for cleaning and packaging are also goals. By showing concern, chefs and restaurant owners become accountable for their role in our well-being and that of our planet.

MINDFUL EATING

We live in a hectic, fast-paced world with many—sometimes too many—choices. By creating an organic kitchen, you play a small but vital part in supporting the ethics of sustainable cuisine. When it comes to shopping, gardening, cooking, and eating, you can make your choices with deliberate consciousness. At the same time, I believe this should be done with joyfulness. If you spend too much time fretting over foods or worrying about whether you are making the right choices, the sensuality and the beauty of food can be easily forgotten.

Accept the fact that you won't always have access to organic products. Be kind to yourself when you answer the urge for junk food and indulge in something that might be considered unhealthy. I admit that whenever I go to a baseball game, I eat a hot dog loaded with mustard, onions, and relish. I don't chastise myself, because I know that human beings are not perfect and these urges are natural. Indulgences are fine if they are occasional and not a part of our daily lives.

Whenever I travel or stay with friends, I try not to push the organic issue. Years ago, I was adamant, until my older son, Josh, pointed out to me that, at times, I was self-righteous and overzealous. Believing in the benefits of using organic, clean foods doesn't give us the right to impose these beliefs on others. This approach rarely works anyway. It is better to lead through example.

I've spent my life trying to eat right and prepare the best possible foods for my family, my friends, and my restaurant patrons. I continue to applaud and support organic farmers who commit to growing the healthiest and, in my opinion, the best-tasting food in the world.

You, too, have a wonderful opportunity to save the environment and preserve the health of your family. It all starts with a shopping cart.

ABOUT THIS BOOK

Since I am passionate about eating locally and seasonally, I have arranged the recipes by season, from Early Spring to Deep Winter. I like to think of the year as a cycle of eight seasons, instead of four, because the beginning of each one is so different from the end. Whatever the season is, no matter where you live, you will find great recipes based on the freshest produce available at that time of the year.

Scattered throughout the book are special features titled "Pioneer Profiles." Here I talk about eight leading companies in the field of organic and sustainable food production. The profiles showcase people who began this journey with goals and passions like my own and have been at the forefront of the organic movement. They are my friends and colleagues, but there are many more who have not been mentioned. These eight companies represent but a handful of the dedicated people who toil daily for this great cause.

I did not include any produce farms or companies, as there are too many to mention, but I probably value them the most, and have the utmost respect and support for the fruits and vegetables they put in the hands of us cooks. In my opinion, produce is the most important ingredient in an organic and sustainable kitchen. It is the place to start planning a meal or menu for family or friends. Everyone, from small local backyard growers to big companies who make organic fruits and vegetables available to those with short growing seasons, should be acknowledged. Their tireless efforts, deep dedication, and willingness to persevere in the face of weather and market fluctuations are remarkable. It is my hope and dream that, someday in the near future, farmers, cooks, and teachers will be held in high regard and given the credit that they deserve for preserving community and good health.

I can't possibly share everything there is to know about organics in this book. Although organic cuisine is just real food, the industrialization of organics has brought on a wonderful new frontier. I urge you to continue to learn more about how our food can be grown so it is as healthy as possible for us and the planet. Consult the Organic Resources section (page 238) for more information.

COMING TO TERMS

You will find many terms throughout this book describing how foods are grown, treated, and labeled. Knowing the basics will help you understand the complexity of it all as you continue to learn more about organics and sustainability. Here are explanations of the most common terms:

BIODIVERSITY The variety of the world's plant and animal species and their habitats. A goal of the organic food movement is the protection of the world's biological resources so they can continue to flourish and evolve.

BIODYNAMIC A type of organic farming based on the philosophy of Rudolf Steiner. A central principle of biodynamics is that the farm is like an organism, and therefore should be a closed, self-nourishing system. The system is nourished by organic practices such as soil preparation.

COMMUNITY-SUPPORTED AGRICULTURE (CSA) A CSA is a paid subscription to a farm in which the members buy a share of its produce. For that share they receive a variety of fruits and/or vegetables throughout the farm's growing season. Often, members can work on the farm as part of their payment.

GENETIC ENGINEERING The use of artificial tissues, organs, or organ components to create genetically modified organisms (GMOs). According to the National Organic Standards Board (NOSB), GMOs are "made with techniques that alter the molecular or cell biology of an organism by means that are not possible under natural conditions or processes." These organisms are used to replace the natural DNA cells in food so that it will function differently, for example, to make a crop more resistant to a weed killer.

ORGANIC According to the U.S. Department of Agriculture (USDA) definition, organic food is produced by farmers who emphasize the use of renewable resources and the conservation of soil and water to enhance environmental quality for future generations. Organic meat, poultry, eggs, and dairy products come from animals that are given no antibiotics or growth hormones. Organic food is produced without using most conventional pesticides or fertilizers made with synthetic ingredients or sewage sludge. Before a product can be labeled Organic, a government-approved certifier inspects the farm where the food is grown to make sure the farmer is following all the rules necessary to meet USDA organic standards. Companies that handle or process organic food before it gets to your local supermarket or restaurant must be certified, too.

Labeling standards are based on the percentage of organic ingredients in a product. Products labeled 100 Percent Organic must contain only organically produced ingredients (except for water and salt). Products labeled Organic must consist of at least 95 percent organically produced ingredients (again, except for water and salt). Products meeting the requirements for 100 Percent Organic or Organic may display the USDA seal.

Processed products that contain at least 70 percent organic ingredients can be labeled "made with organic ingredients" and list up to three of the ingredients or food groups on the principal display panel. For example, soup made with at least 70 percent organic ingredients and only organic vegetables may be labeled either "made with organic peas, potatoes, and carrots," or "made with organic vegetables." Nothing in these products can be grown with fertilizer made from sewage sludge or treated with ionizing radiation, and the USDA seal cannot be used anywhere on the package. Processed products that contain less than 70 percent organic ingredients cannot use the term "organic," other than to identify the specific ingredients that are organically produced in the ingredients statement.

SUSTAINABLE The definition of sustainable food and cuisine will continue to evolve. It begins with people taking care of how our food is produced, from start to finish, and it is also concerned with treating the people who produce this food well. Sustainable agriculture is about raising food that is healthy for people and animals and does not harm the environment. It's about respect, both for the animals being raised and those raising them. Humane working conditions as well as fair wages for all farmworkers are key elements in sustainable systems. Finally, sustainable agriculture supports and enriches rural communities. It considers the proper disposal of organic waste, including the composting of garden debris and food waste, an integral part of the growing cycle.

In addition to food production, "sustainability" refers to manufacturing, energy production, and land development—just about everything people do on this earth. I like to think of sustainability as leaving the planet in better condition than when you arrived.

TRANSITIONAL When farms are working toward being Certified Organic, they are considered transitional. It takes three years of using standards mandated by the NOSB for the farm to be considered for organic certification.

Now that you've made the decision to convert your kitchen to an organic one, recognize that this can't be done overnight. Pace yourself and celebrate every step along the way. This is a time of tiny triumphs. Little by little, day by day, week by week, add more organic ingredients to your kitchen. Forget the past and don't fret about what you haven't done or can't do. Embrace this transformation as a rebirth, a fresh start in creating a healthier you. Then take a step back and acknowledge all the reasons that prompted you to make this life-changing decision: You want to prepare the healthiest and safest foods available for your family and yourself. You want to do your part to protect the environment. You want to show your support for local organic farmers. Along the way, you will evolve into a compassionate consumer as you consciously make the choice to select foods nurtured in healthy soil and grown without pesticides and other harmful agricultural inputs.

WHERE TO BEGIN

Peruse your kitchen shelves for common ingredients that you use on a regular basis. Make a list of these ingredients. Move on to the refrigerator. You may also want to look through your recipe box for family favorites and list the main ingredients. Complete your list, and then get ready to shop.

Many supermarkets now carry an abundance of organic products. There are even some large natural food supermarkets that carry a high percentage of organic products. Don't worry if neither of these options are available to you. Small local natural food stores do carry many organic products, and there are a growing number of mail-order options available. (Be sure to check the Organic Resources on page 238.)

Start by familiarizing yourself with the organic areas of the market. Some large and small supermarkets have a section dedicated to organic products. Others have one separate area in each aisle, and still others simply scatter organic products among conventionally produced items. Take the time to walk through the store and look for all the organic products available. If you have the inclination, ask the store manager to direct you to the organic sections and thank him for providing them. Encourage him to stock more organic products and be sure to buy them. The more organic products you buy, the more the stores will carry.

With your list in hand, start filling your cart with the many organic products available. Remember, this can be a slow process. You may want to pick up just a few new items each week. When it comes to prepared foods, you will be able to easily stock your cupboards with organic broths, soups, grain mixes, canned beans, nut butters, tomato products, salad dressings, cookies, dips, and chips, to name just a few.

Depending on your store's selection, locating fresh produce may be a bit more challenging. In addition to supermarkets and natural food stores, don't forget about the farmers in your area. Your best bet is to start at your local roadside farm stand or farmers' market. Sometimes, especially when you're buying from small local farms, the products may not always be certified Organic, even if the farmers' growing practices are. It takes growers a minimum of three years to earn this distinction, and they must pass stringent requirements. During the process of becoming certified, these farms are classified as Transitional, which means that they are participating in the clean farming methods of certified Organic farms. I buy as many certified Organic products as I can, but I also buy from transitional producers. After all, we have to start somewhere!

Some small farms may not have the time to do all the paperwork to become certified, but they may still be practicing organic methods, so be sure to ask. Other small farms may follow strict organic practices, but have issues with federal control of organic farming or the costs associated with the National Organic Program. Talk to them about their growing methods, buy their products if they are practicing organic and/or sustainable methods, and encourage them to become certified, if appropriate. When possible, visiting the farm or place of production is a good way of seeing firsthand how a product is developed. In any case, most farmers are honest and will accurately represent their farming practices when asked.

Many communities now have farms or groups of farms called Community-Supported Agriculture, or CSA farms (see page 18). These are an ideal way to buy seasonal organic produce. CSA farms fill boxes or bags with whatever is growing locally and seasonally. You often don't know what will be in the box from week to week. Half of the fun is anticipating what will be in your next delivery. You might get items that you wouldn't even consider buying. Celebrate this opportunity to experience new and truly seasonal foods. The farms often provide recipes for each fruit or vegetable; if not, I hope that you will be inspired by some of mine in this cookbook. Or, search the Internet for the fresh item and find a recipe that sounds appealing to you and your family.

Purchasing organic meats, poultry, fish, and dairy products can be a bit more confusing than buying produce. Here's some basic information to help you.

Meat and Poultry

As a cook with a conscience, I keep evolving. I like meat, but I want to know how the animals have been treated before cooking with them. In addition to the usual beef, lamb, and pork, I love when a hunter friend offers me cuts of elk or venison, or wild birds. The flavors are richer and more genuine. I have recently discovered bison (buffalo) and highly recommend it as a substitute for most beef recipes. In general, buffalo is free-roaming, grass-fed, and has not been treated with growth hormones or antibiotics. Because it is so lean, you can cut the cooking time by almost half. Buffalo steaks or burgers cooked rare or medium-rare are absolutely delicious.

In the days before most meat was portioned into plastic trays at supermarkets, people honored the sacrifice of an animal by gratefully eating it all. When I was growing up, my uncle owned a slaughterhouse, and we learned to eat all parts of the animal. Some of my favorite memories are of homemade pickled tongue and sweetbreads grilled on the barbecue. In my restaurants and in my home, I work creatively to cook as many cuts of an animal as I can. Ranchers and farmers struggle when the trend is to eat only one part of an animal, such as the breast of a chicken, or the loin of lamb or beef. There is now renewed interest in eating the whole animal, and hopefully we will all move beyond buying only fillets and chops. I have often pointed out, during speaking engagements, that part of getting ourselves to appreciate real food again is realizing that chickens have not only white meat, but also legs, thighs, and wings.

When possible, buy meat from local farmers. But first, find out how the animals are grazed, fed, and treated, because these factors affect the quality of the meat you eat. If you have a large freezer, contract with a local farmer and buy the whole animal.

Fortunately, Organic certification standards exist for meat and poultry products. For farmers and ranchers to earn certification, their animals must graze on organic fields and eat all-organic diets. The animals must be raised from birth without the use of growth hormones or antibiotics. When shopping in a market, look for products with the Organic certification seal. If these aren't available, your next best choice is to find meat that comes from animals that are ethically raised and free of growth hormones and antibiotics. This information should be prominently displayed on the package. Speak to the butcher in your market and ask how the meat is raised, fed, aged, and butchered.

Farmers have found they can get top dollar for producing meats and poultry without the use of antibiotics and growth hormones, but not all of them practice respectful animal husbandry methods. Some animals, such as pigs, are so confined that the animal never even touches the ground. In addition, one company's definition of "respectful" may vary from another's. So, again, I urge you to ask your butcher questions. Ask how the animals are raised; how much time they spend out of doors, if any; how the grass they eat has been treated; and the type of feed they've consumed.

Here are some definitions of key terms:

NATURAL indicates how livestock is raised. Naturally raised meats and poultry come from animals that have been raised from birth without the use of antibiotics, added growth hormones, growth promotants, or animal by-products in any feed rations.

Organic meats and poultry come from animals that have been raised from birth without the use of antibiotics, added growth hormones, growth promotants, or animal by-products in any feed rations. In addition, they must be fed only certified Organic grasses and/or grains. All animals and feeds must be raised on certified Organic farms and ranches.

GRASS-FED is a term used to signify that livestock have been raised from birth strictly on a grass and/or a forage diet. In other words, grass-fed livestock do not consume grains as part of their diet. Since "grass-fed" specifically addresses the animal's diet, it does not necessarily mean that the meat would qualify for Natural or Organic labels. (Beef labeled Grass-Fed could, for example, come from animals that grazed on fertilized lands, and received antibiotics or growth hormones.) So be sure to look for Grass-Fed Natural, or Grass-Fed Organic for the cleanest products.

"Free-range" is a term that applies to chickens, and in theory it is good for them. However, the designation Free-Range means only that a bird has spent a minimum of two and a half hours a day out of its pen. It does not guarantee that the bird was organically or naturally raised or that it was treated humanely. Again, ask questions.

PASTURE-RAISED refers to animals raised on open land, with space to graze and natural grasses to feed on. These animals may spend time in corrals or enclosures, but they live most of their lives in natural environments.

Fish and Seafood

Currently, there is no certification for organic fish. To certify seafood or fish as Organic would mean imposing controls that would put the fish in some sort of confinement. To do that and ensure that the method used was sustainable for the environment and healthy for humans would be challenging. I recommend that you use sustainably harvested fish and seafood whenever possible. I say this with a note of caution. Learn about the environment where the fish or seafood comes from. Make sure it comes from clean, healthy waters, such as those in Alaska or Iceland. Eating fish as soon as possible after it is caught or harvested is best. Sometimes, that means using fish that has been frozen immediately after being caught.

With the dwindling number of wild fish in our waters and shifts in sea temperatures, however, you may be selecting fish raised in fish farms. Ask questions. Using farm-raised fish is a healthy option only if you are satisfied with how the fish are raised and handled after harvesting. The Monterey Bay Aquarium has a Seafood Watch program, which provides information about edible fish. They promote sustainable fishing and farming methods and have created a useful seafood guide that lists the best and worst options for consumers in every region of the country. Visit their Web site often for the most up-to-date information (www.montereybayaquarium.org/cr/seafoodwatch.asp).

Wild Game

Wild game is, of course, caught in the wild. These animals live and feed naturally off the environment. This doesn't necessarily mean that their meat is organic, but the animals will not have received antibiotics or growth hormones. Depending on where they grazed, they may be as clean as organic animals, so wild game is a good choice.

Eggs

I love raising chickens. They create great compost and eat leftover scraps, and there is nothing that compares to a freshly gathered egg. A few years ago, the coop, which was built around an old tree, went down in a storm. We are building a movable coop, so the chickens can graze on open space (urban chickens can't run wild!). If I am lucky, someone will convince me that I have to buy a little tractor to move it from place to place.

In your quest for organic eggs, remember that the egg comes from the chicken, so organic eggs are simply eggs from organically raised chickens. The color of eggs is determined by the variety of the chicken, nothing more. So, again, select eggs that have earned Organic certification.

Dairy

Organic milk is readily available. If your market does not carry it, request that it do so. The cows, goats, and sheep that produce organic milk should graze on organic grasses and never receive growth hormones or antibiotics. Again, as farmers jump on the organic bandwagon, we need to ask many questions to be sure their cows are being raised with respectful methods. When you've found a producer you are comfortable with, look for their other organic dairy products, such as butter, sour cream, yogurt, and cheese.

Make shopping for organic foods a new and fun experience. Remember to take your time and try various products, until you find the perfect ones for your table. And no matter where you live, take into consideration that you probably won't have year-round access to every organic ingredient you want. Pace yourself and enjoy the process. Over time, your pantry will be a healthy, organic one.

Without question, the surest way to determine if food is organic is to look for a symbol of certification from the USDA's National Organic Standards Board. On processed foods, these symbols are displayed on the label or package, often on the front, so that you will know immediately that it is certified Organic.

But let the buyer beware! Just as the word "lite" is used as a marketing tool (it doesn't necessarily mean that a food contains less fat), a label with just the word "organic" does not guarantee that the food is indeed organically grown. Many of us already read labels for calories and fat content. Apply those same scrutinizing skills in your search for authentic organic products. Look for an Organic seal on the package, and as you scan the ingredients list, look to see what percentage are organic. Remember that "organic" is not a pesticide-free guarantee. After more than fifty years of heavy pesticide use, almost all of our food has some level of pesticide residue. (It's really a matter of how closely we look.) In order to ensure that we eventually reduce the amount of pesticides and toxins in the environment, buy organic today.

As for claims such as "no drugs or growth hormones used," "free-range," and "sustainably harvested," which you may see advertised on a container or package, we all hope that these are honest claims. At the moment, however, there are no specific legal restrictions for using these terms, other than truth-in-labeling or -advertising laws.

Some conventionally grown foods are treated with more pesticides than others. Some retain more of the pesticides. Here's a list of the top twelve foods containing the most pesticides, according to the Environmental Working Group, a nonprofit research group based in Washington, D.C. They call these the "Dirty Dozen."

You can sidestep harm and still eat vitamin-rich foods. If you cannot find these foods raised organically, here are some great alternatives that contain similar vitamins and minerals.

High-Pesticide Food	Main Nutrient	Healthy Alternatives
Apples	Vitamin C	Watermelon, bananas, oranges, tangerines
Bell peppers	Vitamin C	Green peas, broccoli, romaine lettuce
Celery	Potassium	Apricots, avocados, raw mushrooms, winter squash
Cherries	Vitamins A and C	Oranges, blueberries, raspberries, kiwifruit, blackberries, grapefruit
Grapes (imported)	Flavonoids	Peanuts, peanut butter
Lettuce	Vitamins A and K	Chard, kale, collard and mustard greens
Nectarines	Vitamins A and C	Watermelon, tangerines, grapefruit, oranges
Peaches	Vitamins A and C	Watermelon, tangerines, oranges, grapefruit
Pears	Vitamin C	Oranges, bananas, tangerines, berries
Potatoes	Vitamins C and B_6	Broccoli, cauliflower, bananas
Spinach	Vitamins A and K	Chard, kale, collard and mustard greens
Strawberries	Vitamin C	Blueberries, raspberries, oranges, grapefruit, kiwifruit, watermelon

If nonorganic is your only choice, the following have the least amount of pesticides according to the Environmental Working Group's research:

onions   avocados   asparagus   mangoes   kiwifruit   bananas

FIRST OF SPRING

By the time winter nears its end, I am ready, waiting, and hungry for the treasures of spring to shoot up from the moist, cool soil. The spring rains, interrupted only by glimpses of sunshine, yield tender yet full-flavored greens, tiny sweet lettuces, pea shoots, asparagus, artichokes, and wild mushrooms. Sugar snap peas and spring onions follow, inspiring the creation of lighter dishes from my organic kitchen. | Asparagus remains the star, and for good reason. There are few vegetables that rival its popularity and versatility at this time of the year. Whether they're steamed and eaten chilled with a garlicky dip, tossed in salads, puréed into soups, grilled on the barbecue, or wrapped in salty meats, many of us just can't seem to get enough of these tender spears. | Next on my prized list for early spring is the artichoke. I remember the days when it was next to impossible to find organic artichokes. To satisfy our cravings, my son Jonah and I would treat ourselves to nonorganic artichokes. We regarded them as our "must-have junk food." These days, more artichokes are grown organically, so we eat them often. Early spring is a time that beckons me back to the farmers' market after a long, dormant winter. Whether or not there is a farmers' market open near you, this is a good time of the year to become reacquainted with local farmers, fishermen, ranchers, cheese makers, and bread bakers—the people who grow and produce your food.

PEA AND POTATO CAKES

This is a great way to use up leftover mashed potatoes. If your leftovers are made with butter or milk, omit the cheese and add a little more flour to bind them. Always test a small cake first for consistency. Peas and potatoes are as good as it gets, but instead of peas, you can use bits of any delicate summer or winter vegetable, or a more robust one that has been cooked until very tender.

¾ pound fresh peas, shelled
    (about ¾ cup)

4 tablespoons olive oil

1 large onion, thinly sliced

2 garlic cloves, minced

2 cups cooked mashed potatoes

1 cup shredded Cheddar cheese
    (about 4 ounces)

3 tablespoons unbleached
    all-purpose flour

½ teaspoon salt

¼ teaspoon freshly ground black
    pepper

4 cups mesclun or spring salad mix

1 large carrot, shaved into curls
    with a peeler

In a small saucepan, bring 1 inch of water to a boil over high heat. Add the peas and blanch for 2 minutes. Drain, put in a medium bowl, and cool slightly.

Wipe the saucepan clean and heat 1 tablespoon of the olive oil over medium heat. Add the onion and cook for 4 minutes, or until soft. Add the garlic and cook for 2 minutes. Place in a large bowl and cool slightly.

Add the peas, potatoes, cheese, flour, salt, and pepper to the bowl. Stir until well-blended. Shape into 8 round cakes.

Heat 1½ tablespoons of the remaining olive oil in the same skillet over medium heat. Add 4 cakes and cook for 8 minutes, turning once, or until browned and heated through. Transfer the cakes to a plate and keep warm. Repeat with the remaining 4 cakes.

Divide the mesclun and carrot curls evenly among 4 plates and top with the cakes.

VARIATIONS
This recipe is quite flexible. Try using sweet potatoes instead of the white, and fresh asparagus instead of the peas.

HERB-STUFFED ARTICHOKES

This recipe was inspired by my love of fresh goat cheese from one of our favorite local producers, Harley Farms, in the Santa Cruz Mountains of California. Artichokes are not easy to grow organically, so when we can find them, we buy as many as our hands can hold.

4 medium artichokes

8 ounces soft goat cheese, such as chèvre

2 tablespoons dry bread crumbs

2 garlic cloves, minced

2 tablespoons chopped fresh chives

1 tablespoon chopped fresh oregano

Salt

Freshly ground black pepper

1 tablespoon olive oil

Juice of 1 large lemon

Put a steamer basket in a large pot and add 2 inches of water. Bring to a boil over high heat.

Using scissors, trim off the sharp tips of the outer leaves of the artichokes. Put the artichokes in the steamer basket and steam for 25 to 35 minutes, or until tender. Turn the steamer upside down over a plate to remove the artichokes, and cool slightly.

Preheat the oven to 375°F. Gently open the center of each artichoke. Using a teaspoon, remove and discard the inner chokes and thistles.

In a small bowl, combine the cheese, bread crumbs, garlic, chives, and oregano. Season with salt and pepper. Divide the cheese mixture evenly among the cavities of the artichokes. Press the leaves back in place and rub gently with the oil. Season generously with the salt and pepper, and sprinkle the lemon juice over the artichokes.

Place the artichokes in a shallow pan and bake for 15 minutes, or until heated through. Cut each artichoke in half. To eat, dip the leaves into the cheese mixture.

EXOTIC MUSHROOM SOUP

At Flea St. Café, we are lucky enough to have as a friend Todd Spanier, the king of mushrooms, who brings us treasures through the back door of our kitchen. This simple recipe works with both wild mushrooms and domestic buttons. If it seems wasteful to use a lot of expensive wild mushrooms in soup, but you don't want to sacrifice those deep, enticing flavors, try a combination of wild and domestic.

3 tablespoons olive oil

1 onion, finely chopped

1½ pounds wild or domestic mushrooms, or a combination, cleaned and coarsely chopped

¼ cup Madeira or cream sherry

⅓ cup unbleached all-purpose flour

5 cups vegetable or chicken broth

1 cup sour cream

2 to 3 tablespoons chopped fresh Italian parsley

1 teaspoon paprika

Salt

Freshly ground black pepper

Warm the oil in a large saucepan over medium heat. Add the onion and mushrooms and cook, stirring occasionally, for 7 minutes, or until very soft. Add the Madeira and cook for 2 minutes. Sprinkle with the flour and continue cooking, stirring constantly, for 3 minutes. Gradually add the broth and simmer, stirring occasionally, for 5 minutes, or until the soup thickens slightly.

Add the sour cream, parsley, and paprika. Cook, stirring occasionally, for 3 minutes, or until heated through. Season with salt and pepper to taste.

KITCHEN TIP

Any blend of mushrooms works well. I like shiitakes mixed with regular button mushrooms. When wild mushrooms are available, consider a combination of the somewhat mild chanterelles with porcini or other full-flavored mushrooms.

ASPARAGUS AND SCALLOPS

This is a perfect dish for springtime, served with fresh rolls and a crisp white wine.

3 tablespoons extra-virgin olive oil

3 tablespoons fresh lime juice

2 tablespoons sugar

2 garlic cloves, minced

1 whole canned chipotle chile pepper, puréed or minced

3 tablespoons finely chopped fresh cilantro

1 pound sea scallops

¾ cup yellow cornmeal

1 teaspoon ground coriander

½ teaspoon salt

¼ teaspoon freshly ground black pepper

1 pound asparagus, trimmed

2 tablespoons unsalted butter

Lime wedges for garnish

In a small bowl, combine the oil, lime juice, sugar, garlic, chile pepper, and cilantro. Let sit for at least 30 minutes.

Remove and discard the tough muscle from the scallops.

In a small bowl, combine the cornmeal, coriander, salt, and black pepper. Toss the scallops in the cornmeal mixture and set aside.

Pour ½ cup water into a heavy skillet. Bring to a boil over high heat. Add the asparagus. Reduce the heat to medium-low, cover, and simmer for 4 minutes, or until tender-crisp. Remove to a platter and keep warm.

Wipe the skillet and add the butter. Place over medium heat to melt the butter. Add the scallops and cook for 2 to 4 minutes, turning once, until lightly browned and opaque.

Divide the asparagus evenly among 4 plates. Top with the scallops. Drizzle with the chipotle dressing, and garnish with lime wedges.

KITCHEN TIP

Often scallops are soaked in sodium tripolyphosphate (STP) to help keep them moist. To avoid chemical-laden scallops, look for scallops labeled Day Boat, Diver, Dry Pack, or Chemical-Free. These scallops are more readily available these days and, of course, are a much healthier choice. They may not be perfectly white and uniform in size, but those qualities are not natural to scallops; they are human-induced. As always, opt for the most natural products available. And, as always, ask questions. The fishmonger should know exactly where the fish is from and how it has been treated.

LASAGNA WITH CHARD

When my oldest son, Joshua, was young, he loved this tomato-less lasagna. It was a great substitute for the more traditional version during the winter, when tomatoes weren't in season. It became a year-round favorite because of its luscious appeal. Around the holidays, when we felt like splurging, we mounded fresh crabmeat on top.

12 ounces lasagna noodles

2 tablespoons olive oil

4 cups firmly packed, very thinly sliced red or green chard

2 shallots, minced

2 tablespoons unbleached all-purpose flour

4 cups milk

¼ teaspoon freshly grated nutmeg

½ cup grated Parmesan cheese (about 2 ounces)

1 pound ricotta cheese

8 ounces mozzarella cheese, cut into small chunks

½ cup grated hard Jack cheese (about 2 ounces)

1 large egg, beaten

2 tablespoons chopped fresh oregano

3 tablespoons chopped fresh Italian parsley

½ teaspoon salt

¼ teaspoon freshly ground black pepper

Preheat the oven to 375°F. Lightly coat a 13-by-9-inch baking dish with oil.

Cook the lasagna noodles in a large pot of boiling water according to package directions. Drain and rinse under cold water. Drain thoroughly.

While the pasta is cooking, heat the oil in a medium saucepan over medium heat. Add the chard and shallots and cook for 4 minutes, or until soft. Using a slotted spoon, remove to a large bowl. Whisk the flour into the liquid remaining in the pan and cook, stirring frequently, for 3 minutes. Gradually whisk in the milk and cook, stirring often, for 15 minutes, or until the sauce reaches a simmer and thickens. Stir in the chard, shallots, nutmeg, and Parmesan. Simmer for 1 minute.

In a medium bowl, combine the ricotta, mozzarella, hard Jack, egg, oregano, parsley, salt, and pepper.

Spread one-quarter of the chard sauce on the bottom of the prepared baking dish. Layer one-third of the lasagna noodles on the sauce. Spread one-third of the ricotta mixture on top of the lasagna. Spread another one-quarter of the sauce over the cheese mixture. Repeat with the remaining lasagna, ricotta, and sauce.

Bake for 45 minutes, or until golden brown on top and heated through. Let stand for 10 minutes before serving.

CHICKEN WITH GREENS AND SPRING ONIONS

In the spring, when I'm thinning beds of all kinds of greens, I like to steam them rather than tossing them into the compost. I mix them with slow-cooked onions and slip the mixture under the skin of chicken breasts or thighs. The juices seep into the meat, enhancing the flavor and adding moisture.

1 small chicken (2½ to 3 pounds), whole or cut into parts

4 tablespoons extra-virgin olive oil

2 cups coarsely chopped spring onion (green and white parts)

2 garlic cloves, minced

6 cups firmly packed, coarsely chopped greens, such as tatsoi, mizuna, arugula, or spinach

⅓ cup chopped fresh dill

2 teaspoons salt, plus extra for seasoning

1 teaspoon freshly ground black pepper, plus extra for seasoning

3 tablespoons herbes de Provence

Rinse the chicken under cold water, pat dry, and set aside in the refrigerator in a baking dish.

Preheat the oven to 400°F.

In a medium skillet, heat 3 tablespoons of the olive oil over medium heat, add the onions and garlic and cook until soft, about 5 minutes. Add the greens and dill and toss well.

Reduce the heat, cover, and cook for about 3 minutes, or until the greens are wilted.

Remove from the heat. With a slotted spoon, transfer the greens to a bowl to cool, seasoning well with salt and pepper. Reserve any juices.

Pull the skin back from the chicken and stuff the cooked greens under the skin.

In a small bowl, combine the herbes de Provence, the 2 teaspoons salt, 1 teaspoon pepper, and the remaining 1 tablespoon oil. Rub the mixture over the chicken.

Place the chicken in a roasting pan and add the reserved juices from the greens. Roast in the oven until a thermometer inserted in the thigh joint registers 175°F, about 15 to 20 minutes per pound for a whole chicken, and a total of 45 minutes to 1 hour for cut-up chicken.

Let the chicken stand for 15 minutes before serving. Skim off the fat from the pan juices and pour the juices over the chicken as a sauce.

ORGANIC TIP

Whenever possible, opt for free-range, pasture-raised organic chicken; it is worth the extra cost. It is best, when possible, to buy a whole chicken and use all the parts. In general, we want to try to use as much of an animal as possible.

QUAIL WITH PRESERVED LEMONS

Before the industrialization of poultry, the wilder, more sustainable approach was to hunt game birds and eat what you brought home. We also didn't think that the breast meat was the only desirable part. A more holistic approach to eating game birds such as quail, or any animal for that matter, is to find ways to eat the entire animal. And give gratitude for the opportunity.

4 quail or other small game birds

1 cup red wine

5 whole peppercorns, crushed with the side of a knife

2 tablespoons coarsely chopped fresh rosemary

3 to 4 garlic cloves, minced

½ cup olive oil, plus extra for drizzling

Salt

Freshly ground black pepper

4 wedges preserved lemon (about ½ lemon), rinsed and finely chopped (see Kitchen Tip)

2 tablespoons chopped fresh Italian parsley

Pinch of ground red pepper (cayenne)

½ cup olives

Rinse the birds under cold water and pat dry. In a medium bowl, combine the wine, peppercorns, rosemary, half of the garlic, and 2 tablespoons of the olive oil. Season the birds with salt and pepper and marinate for at least 4 hours or overnight.

In a medium bowl, combine the preserved lemon, parsley, the remaining 6 tablespoons oil, the remaining garlic, and salt, pepper, and ground red pepper to taste. Set aside at room temperature.

Prepare a hot charcoal fire, preheat a gas grill on high, or preheat the broiler. Remove the quail from the marinade and pat dry. Grill or broil on an oiled rack, 5 to 6 inches from the heat source,

for 6 to 8 minutes, turning once, until the juices run clear when a thigh is pierced. Or you can cook the quail in a hot grill pan.

Place 1 quail on each plate and spoon the preserved lemon mixture and olives generously over the quail.

KITCHEN TIP

Preserved lemons are easy to make. Simply cut several whole lemons into wedges, cover with as much sea salt as you can, and literally cram the wedges into a jar. You can't use too much salt. The lemon wedges are ready to use when they are very soft. It takes about 2 weeks.

LAMB CHOPS WITH STRAWBERRY–RHUBARB SAUCE

These lamb chops are wonderful with steamed rice tossed with slivered almonds and chopped chives.

4 rib or loin lamb chops (about 2½ ounces each)

2 garlic cloves, minced

2 tablespoons finely chopped fresh rosemary

¼ teaspoon salt

¼ teaspoon freshly ground black pepper

2 teaspoons olive oil

½ small red onion, thinly sliced

4 ounces rhubarb, thinly sliced

2 tablespoons ruby port or balsamic vinegar

¾ cup sliced strawberries

¼ cup sugar

¼ teaspoon freshly grated nutmeg

Preheat the broiler.

Put the chops on a broiler pan and rub with the garlic, rosemary, salt, and pepper. Set aside.

Heat the oil in a medium saucepan over medium heat. Add the onion and cook for 5 minutes, or until soft. Add the rhubarb and cook for 6 minutes, or until the rhubarb is soft. Add the port or vinegar and cook for 2 minutes, or until the liquid is absorbed by the rhubarb. Add the strawberries, sugar, and nutmeg. Reduce the heat to low and simmer for 5 minutes, or until the sauce is well blended.

Meanwhile, broil the chops, turning once, for a total of 5 minutes, or until browned and a thermometer inserted in the center registers 145°F for medium-rare.

Serve the chops with the sauce.

FILET MIGNON WITH SMASHED POTATOES AND LEEK SAUCE

This steak is very easy to prepare and a great dish for an impressive meal for a dinner party.

4 filet mignon steaks (about 5 ounces
    each)

½ teaspoon salt

2 tablespoons coarsely ground black
    pepper

1 pound new potatoes

¼ to ½ cup buttermilk (see Organic Tip)

3 tablespoons chopped fresh chives

3 tablespoons olive oil

2 large leeks (white part only), sliced

½ cup hearty red wine, such as
    Zinfandel or Cabernet

1 tablespoon capers

1 tablespoon chopped fresh tarragon

2 tablespoons chopped fresh Italian
    parsley

Prepare a hot charcoal fire or preheat a gas grill on high, or preheat the broiler. Lightly oil the grill rack or broiler pan.

Rub the steaks with the salt, then press the pepper into both sides. Set aside.

Bring a large pot of salted water to a boil. Add the potatoes and cook for 15 minutes, or until tender. Drain and put in a large bowl. Mash the potatoes with a potato masher or fork, adding enough buttermilk so they are moist. Add the chives, cover, and keep warm.

While the potatoes are cooking, heat the olive oil in a medium saucepan over medium heat. Add the leeks and cook for 6 minutes, or until very soft. Add the wine, capers, and tarragon. Simmer for 3 minutes, or until well blended and heated through. Keep warm.

Grill or broil the steaks, turning once, for a total of 6 minutes, or until a thermometer inserted in the center registers 145°F for medium-rare.

To serve, divide the potatoes and steaks evenly among 4 plates. Top with the sauce and sprinkle with the parsley.

KITCHEN TIPS

You can buy coarsely ground pepper, but when the peppercorns are freshly ground, the flavor is superior. I like to use a combination of red, green, and black peppercorns. Look for this mix, often sold as "peppercorn mélange," in most supermarkets.

Smashed potatoes are much coarser than creamy mashed ones and always include the skin as well as the potato flesh. They're not only delicious, but nutritious as well.

ORGANIC TIP

Organic buttermilk isn't as easy to find as regular organic milk. If your grocer doesn't carry it, you can substitute sour milk. To make sour milk, add 1 tablespoon vinegar to 1 cup milk and let sit for 10 minutes.

SPRING VEGETABLE SAUTÉ

For me, spring has really begun when I go to the market and find sugar snap peas. In a basket nearby, there are often new potatoes and fragrant spring onions. Bringing them together in a dish as simple as this seems only natural.

12 ounces new potatoes, halved

8 ounces sugar snap peas, trimmed

2 tablespoons unsalted butter

3 to 4 small spring onions with greens, thinly sliced

2 garlic cloves, minced

½ teaspoon freshly grated nutmeg

2 to 3 tablespoons chopped fresh mint

Salt

Freshly ground black pepper

Place a large pot of salted water over high heat and bring to a boil. Add the potatoes and cook for 20 minutes, or until tender. Add the snap peas during the last 2 minutes of the cooking time. Drain the pot and wipe it clean.

Heat the butter in the same pot over medium heat. Add the onions and garlic and cook for 5 minutes, or until tender. Add the potatoes, snap peas, nutmeg, and mint. Toss to coat well. Season with salt and pepper to taste and serve.

ORGANIC TIP

Spring onions look like the green onions commonly found in your produce department, and have a similar, yet fresher, flavor. Both are immature shoots before an onion bulbs. Commercially grown green onions are bred for consistency and durability. Spring or garden fresh green onions are sweeter and more true to a fresh, mild onion flavor.

STEAMED BOK CHOY AND WATER CHESTNUTS

At times, I like vegetables cooked until they are very soft, forming a soup of sorts with a savory yet often simple broth. The broth adds dimension and flavor without relying on olive oil or butter. There is often a container of this comforting health food in my refrigerator.

1½ pounds bok choy

2 cups vegetable or chicken broth

2 garlic cloves, minced

1 small onion, thinly sliced

½ orange (unpeeled), cut into wedges

1 can (4 ounces) sliced water chestnuts, drained

½ cup chopped fresh cilantro

2 tablespoons tamari or soy sauce

Salt

Freshly ground black pepper

If the bok choy heads are small, cut into halves or quarters. If it is one large head, chop into bite-size pieces.

In a medium saucepan over high heat, bring the broth, garlic, onion, and orange wedges to a boil. Reduce the heat to low, cover, and simmer for 5 minutes. Add the bok choy and simmer for 5 minutes, or until tender. Add the water chestnuts, cilantro, and tamari or soy sauce. Simmer for 1 minute. Remove and discard the orange wedges.

Season the vegetables with salt and pepper to taste. Serve in bowls.

BABY ARTICHOKE, PARSLEY, AND CELERY SALAD

Artichokes and celery are wonderful together. This light and refreshing salad is the perfect accompaniment to pasta dishes. Do not be afraid to cut away and discard the tough, leafy parts of the artichoke. Trying to chew them is far worse.

2 ½ pounds baby artichokes

⅓ cup fresh lemon juice

1 cup thinly sliced celery

1 medium red onion, or 5 green onions, thinly sliced

1 cup packed whole Italian parsley, stems removed

¼ cup capers

⅓ cup extra-virgin olive oil

Dash of Tabasco

Salt

Freshly ground black pepper

To clean the artichokes, first pull away and discard the outer leaves until all that remains is the very light, tender inside leaves. Using a sharp knife, cut off and discard the tips of the remaining leaves and all the dark parts.

Pour the lemon juice into a large bowl. Slice the trimmed artichokes thinly and add to the lemon juice, tossing well. Add the celery, onion, parsley, capers, oil, Tabasco, and salt and pepper to taste.

Serve the salad at room temperature or transfer to a skillet and cook over medium heat for 2 minutes to warm slightly.

KITCHEN TIP
Unlike mature artichokes, baby artichokes have no chokes to remove.

FENNEL AND APRICOT SALAD

Simple yet flavorful, this salad improves overnight, so try to make it a day ahead.

3 tablespoons extra-virgin olive oil

Juice of 1 lemon

2 tablespoons chopped fresh thyme

2 tablespoons honey

¼ teaspoon salt

¼ teaspoon freshly ground black pepper

1 large fennel bulb, shaved very thin

1 small red onion, shaved very thin

3 apricots

In a medium bowl, whisk together the oil, lemon juice, thyme, honey, salt, and pepper. Add the fennel and onion, and marinate at room temperature for at least 1 hour.

Just before serving, pit and thinly slice the apricots, and add them to the fennel and onions. Adjust the seasoning and serve.

VARIATIONS

Use celery in place of the fennel, or try a combination of both. If fresh apricots are not yet in season, use about 2 ounces dried apricots, thinly sliced. Add them to the dressing when you add the fennel and onions.

SPRING GREENS, ONIONS, AND CHIVES WITH HERB BUTTER–RADISH TOASTS

For me, this dish is the essence of springtime. The salad would make a wonderful bed, nestled beneath roast chicken or grilled sausages. The rich toasts, eaten out of hand, complete the peasant-style meal.

1½ pounds mixed salad greens: sweet, bitter, and spicy

⅓ cup extra-virgin olive oil

3 tablespoons balsamic vinegar

1 tablespoon tamari or soy sauce

2 tablespoons brown sugar

2 garlic cloves, minced

2 green onions, thinly sliced

½ cup (1 stick) unsalted butter, softened

2 tablespoons chopped fresh chives

2 tablespoons chopped fresh tarragon

1 small loaf whole grain Italian bread, cut diagonally into 12 slices about 1 inch thick and toasted

6 radishes, thinly sliced

Salt

Freshly ground black pepper

Wash and dry the greens and put them in a large mixing bowl. In a small bowl, combine the oil, vinegar, tamari or soy sauce, brown sugar, garlic, and green onions.

In another small bowl, combine the butter, chives, and tarragon. Spread the bread slices with the herb butter. Arrange the radishes on top and season with a little salt and pepper.

Season the greens with salt and pepper and moisten to your liking with the vinaigrette. (Refrigerate any remaining vinaigrette for up to 2 weeks.)

Mound the salad on a larger platter or individual plates. Serve with the toasts.

RASPBERRY MILLET PANCAKES

MAKES

6

SERVINGS

We all like warm desserts right out of the oven. An easy and quick way to make a sweet cake to order is in the form of a pancake. If you have a big sweet tooth, add more maple syrup or even sugar to the batter. Serve with sour cream or vanilla frozen yogurt or ice cream.

⅓ cup millet

2 large eggs

1½ cups buttermilk (see Organic Tip on page 38)

¼ cup pure maple syrup

2 tablespoons vegetable oil

1 teaspoon vanilla extract

1½ cups whole grain pastry flour

1½ teaspoons baking soda

1 teaspoon ground cinnamon

½ teaspoon salt

1 pint raspberries

1 pint vanilla frozen yogurt

Put the millet in a medium saucepan over medium heat. Toast the grains, shaking the pan often, for 3 minutes, or until lightly browned. Add 1 cup water and bring to a boil over high heat. Reduce the heat to low, cover, and simmer for 15 minutes, or until the liquid is absorbed. Remove from the heat, but do not remove the cover, and let stand for 15 minutes. Cool to room temperature.

Meanwhile, in a medium bowl, combine the eggs, buttermilk, maple syrup, oil, and vanilla extract.

In a large bowl, combine the flour, baking soda, cinnamon, and salt. Form a well in the center of the flour mixture, pour in the buttermilk mixture, and stir to incorporate the dry ingredients into the wet just until blended. Add the millet, stirring to blend.

Lightly oil a griddle or large skillet and heat over medium-high heat. Drop the batter by scant ¼ cups onto the pan. Cook for 3 minutes, or until the uncooked side begins to bubble. Flip over and cook for 2 minutes, or until browned.

To serve, place 3 pancakes on each plate. Top with the raspberries and frozen yogurt.

DRIED CRANBERRY– RICOTTA DESSERT PUDDING

This unusual dessert, which is like a cheesecake, also appeals to me for breakfast and for a midnight snack while I watch late-night TV.

½ cup dried cranberries

3 large eggs

1½ pounds ricotta cheese

1 cup plain low-fat yogurt

½ cup sugar

1 teaspoon vanilla extract

½ teaspoon freshly grated nutmeg

Preheat the oven to 350°F. Fill a large baking pan with 2 cups water. Butter eight 6-ounce ramekins or one 1-quart baking dish and place them in the pan with the water. Scatter the cranberries on the bottoms of the ramekins or baking dish.

Separate the eggs, putting the whites in a medium bowl and the yolks in a large bowl.

Beat the egg whites with an electric mixer on high speed until soft peaks form. Set aside.

Add the ricotta, yogurt, sugar, and vanilla extract to the bowl with the egg yolks. Using the same beaters, beat the mixture until smooth. Fold the egg whites into the ricotta mixture.

Pour into the prepared ramekins or baking dish. Sprinkle the nutmeg on the top. If using ramekins, bake the pudding for 30 minutes. If using a baking dish, bake for about 45 minutes, or until a knife inserted in the center comes out clean. Cool completely on a rack.

Serve at room temperature or refrigerate to serve cold later.

KITCHEN TIP

This pudding can be adapted to your preferences. For a lighter version, use low-fat ricotta cheese. For a richer pudding, substitute sour cream for the yogurt.

BANANA-WALNUT SHORTBREAD

I like simple desserts, especially versatile ones like these cookies. They can stand on their own, but they are glorious when served alongside bowls of fresh strawberries or chocolate ice cream.

2½ cups whole grain pastry flour

½ teaspoon baking powder

⅛ teaspoon salt

1½ cups (3 sticks) unsalted butter, softened

¾ cup packed brown sugar

1 large very ripe banana, mashed

1 teaspoon vanilla extract

½ cup chopped walnuts

Preheat the oven to 400°F.

In a medium bowl, combine the flour, baking powder, and salt.

In a large bowl, beat the butter and brown sugar with an electric mixer, until creamy. Add the banana and vanilla extract, beating just until incorporated. Add the flour mixture and beat just until well blended. Stir in the nuts.

Divide the dough into quarters. Press one-quarter of the dough into an 8-inch circle on a large baking sheet. Using the dull side of a knife blade, score the dough, creating an outline of 12 pie-shaped wedges. Repeat with a second quarter of the dough on the same baking sheet. Shape the remaining quarters of dough on another large baking sheet.

Bake for 20 minutes, or until the shortbread is lightly browned and has risen. Place on racks to cool and cut into wedges.

STRAWBERRY-CHOCOLATE COBBLER

This standard cobbler recipe makes good use of the first fresh fruit of spring: strawberries. I like to serve it warm with vanilla ice cream and hot fudge sauce.

½ cup (1 stick) unsalted butter

⅓ cup unsweetened cocoa powder

1 cup sugar

2 cups whole grain pastry flour

2 teaspoons baking powder

1 teaspoon ground cinnamon

1 cup milk

1 pint strawberries, hulled and sliced

Preheat the oven to 350°F.

Combine the butter, cocoa, and ¼ cup of the sugar in a 3-quart glass baking dish. Place in the oven for 3 to 5 minutes to melt the butter. Remove from the oven and stir until well blended.

Meanwhile, in a medium bowl, combine the flour, baking powder, cinnamon, and the remaining ¾ cup sugar. Add the milk and stir until the mixture is smooth. Spoon over the melted butter mixture, but do not stir. Scatter the strawberries on top.

Bake for 45 to 55 minutes, or until a wooden pick inserted in the center comes out clean. Let stand for 15 minutes before serving.

SEEDS OF CHANGE

Farmers and backyard gardeners are people for whom I have a huge amount of respect. When you grow your own organic produce, you appreciate the challenges and rewards of seasonal, local production and savor the very best that Mother Earth has to offer.

Although I have always dabbled in gardening, I've only recently begun to really learn how to grow food. My garden is a place where I can test seeds, paying attention to how plants grow and, most important, to how they taste. Seeds of Change is one of the best sources for organic seeds and heirloom varieties.

In 1989, three guys as passionate as I am about changing the direction of food production started Seeds of Change. They wanted to help preserve the planet's biodiversity by cultivating and offering consumers a wide range of open-pollinated, organically grown, heirloom and traditional vegetable, flower, and herb seeds. They encourage all gardeners and farmers to join them in the important work of seed saving and genetic preservation. The company seeks traditional seed varieties from the Americas and treasured heirlooms from abroad. Many of these are in danger of being lost due to rapid consolidation within the seed industry and the decline of indigenous agriculture and seed-saving knowledge. Now Seeds of Change also offers a broad selection of 100-percent-organic seedlings, as well as gardening tools (my remarkable greenhouse came from them), books, and an extensive line of their own organic foods.

The mission of Seeds of Change is as relevant today as it was in 1989. They believe, as I do, that there is a solution to one of our greatest environmental crises: the loss of biodiversity and the erosion and pollution of our precious soil. Our conventional agricultural methods are polluting the planet and our own bodies. They are threatening the health of future generations, as well as squandering our valuable soil, water, and energy resources. Seeds of Change believes we can alter our course, starting with their seeds. I know they already have made a big difference.

LATE SPRING

By mid-April, my mind, my soul, and my taste buds are ready for light, bright spring flavors. Late spring is a time of transition. The pavement is dry, but a hint of coolness remains. The air delivers a fresh, warm, floral scent from the many blooms of roses and edible, colorful flowers. Baby root vegetables like turnips and carrots announce their arrival. | The weather is predictably unpredictable—days waver between rainy and chilly and dry and warm. I find myself catering to these climate changes in my kitchen. On cool, damp days, I am filled with the desire to prepare warm, meaty dishes. When the sun dominates the day, I shift to lighter, fresher fare with flavors on the brink of ripeness. I rejoice in the spring harvest that provides me with the gifts of salad greens, berries, artichokes, mushrooms, and fresh herbs. | The weather also affects me physically. I find it difficult to exercise during cold spring days, rebelliously resisting the gym. I gain a few pounds as I satisfy my craving for fattier foods. On sunny spring days, the outdoors beckons me, and I find myself enthusiastically walking the challenging hills near my home to expend some calories and meditate. | Without a doubt, exercise, diet, and joyfulness are the keys to keeping healthy. Springtime simply makes it easier to keep oneself in balance physically, mentally, and spiritually.

SPRING VEGETABLE WITH ARUGULA PESTO

MAKES
4 TO 6
SERVINGS

Traditional pesto is made with basil using a mortar and pestle, but in my modern kitchen, I use a food processor and have ventured far beyond basil. Flavorful leafy greens and herbs, like arugula or Italian parsley can be gently chopped or ground into a pesto, flavored with fruity olive oil and garlic.

I often leave out the cheese and nuts and add them later as a garnish. This makes the flavor of each ingredient in the pesto distinct.

⅓ cup pine nuts

3 cups chopped spring vegetables, such as carrots, asparagus, potatoes, celeriac, artichokes, and spring onions

1 pound arugula

2 to 3 garlic cloves

½ cup olive oil

Juice of 1 lemon

Salt

Freshly ground black pepper

4 ounces aged cheese, such as Parmigiano-Reggiano, Asiago, hard Jack, or Grana Padano

Toast the pine nuts in a heavy-bottomed sauté pan over medium-high heat, stirring often, until they turn a golden brown. Cool.

Fill a large bowl with water and ice and place next to the stove top. Bring a saucepan of salted water to a boil. Add the vegetables and blanch for 2 minutes, or until they are cooked but still have a little crunch or an invitingly tender texture. Using a slotted spoon, remove to the ice water. Once cooled, remove to a colander to drain.

In a food processor or blender, chop the arugula and garlic as finely as possible. Add enough olive oil to purée. Add the lemon juice and season generously with the salt and pepper. Remove to an airtight container.

Just before serving, arrange the vegetables artfully on a platter.

Either dollop the pesto on top or serve it in a small bowl. Sprinkle the vegetables with the pine nuts and shave plenty of cheese on top.

KITCHEN TIP

When chopping the vegetables, make them as uniform as possible so that all of the carrots, for example, are cooked through at the same time.

When blanching the vegetables, do so in stages, starting with those that take longer to cook or will impart more color or flavor to the cooking water. For this recipe, start with the potatoes, carrots, celeriac, and artichokes, followed by the asparagus and tender young spring onions.

CURRY CARROT SOUP
WITH WASABI CREAM

MAKES
8
SERVINGS

This lovely, bright soup makes perfect use of the first sweet carrots that come out of the ground. I like it prepared as a creamy soup, but it is a bit easier and just as delicious to serve the soup somewhat chunky. Simply omit the puréeing step.

3 tablespoons unsalted butter

2 large onions, thinly sliced

2 pounds carrots, thinly sliced

½ cup mirin cooking wine or apple juice

6 cups vegetable or chicken broth

¼ cup grated fresh ginger

1 tablespoon curry powder

1 to 3 tablespoons honey

Salt

Freshly ground black pepper

1 tablespoon wasabi powder

1 cup sour cream or yogurt

4 green onions, chopped

Melt the butter in a large pot over medium-high heat. Add the onions and cook for 5 minutes, or until soft. Add the carrots and wine or apple juice and cook for 3 minutes. Add the broth, ginger, and curry powder and bring to a boil.

Reduce the heat to low, cover, and simmer for 40 minutes, or until the carrots are very tender.

Remove from the heat. Working in batches, pour the soup into a food processor or blender. Process until smooth. Transfer to a soup tureen or large bowl. Stir in the honey, and salt and pepper to taste.

While the soup is cooking, in a small bowl, blend the wasabi powder with the sour cream or yogurt. Stir in the green onions.

Ladle the soup into bowls and top with a generous spoonful of the wasabi cream. Swirl the cream into the soup.

KITCHEN TIP
For an elegant touch, spoon the wasabi cream into a small pastry bag and pipe the cream onto the soup. Use a wooden pick to create a decorative design.

RICOTTA–GREEN ONION GNOCCHI

MAKES
4
SERVINGS

Gnocchi have become an all-time favorite around my house. I typically make far more than can be eaten at one meal. They freeze well and can be taken from the freezer and dropped directly into boiling water to cook. Try these gnocchi with a simple red sauce or drizzled with olive oil, garlic, parsley, and lots of grated Italian cheese.

15 ounces ricotta cheese

1 large egg, beaten

½ teaspoon salt

½ teaspoon freshly ground black pepper

6 green onions, minced

½ cup grated Asiago or Parmesan cheese (about 2 ounces)

1½ to 2 cups unbleached all-purpose flour

3 cups marinara sauce

Put the ricotta in a sieve and place over a bowl for 15 to 30 minutes to drain. Discard the liquid.

Bring a large pot of salted water to a boil.

In a medium bowl, combine the drained ricotta, egg, salt, pepper, green onions, and Asiago or Parmesan. Gradually add the flour, ¼ cup at a time, using your hands and blending just until the dough holds together. Remove 1 teaspoon of the dough and roll into a ball on a floured surface. Drop into the boiling water. If the piece falls apart, add more flour to the dough, 2 table-spoons at a time, until it will form a ball. Repeat the cooking test until the dough holds together and floats to the surface.

Divide the dough into 4 equal parts. On a generously floured board, using your hands, roll each section into a rope about 1 inch in diameter.

Cut the ropes into 1-inch-long pieces and slightly indent with a fork. If you're not using the gnocchi right away, cover them thoroughly with flour and store in the refrigerator or freezer.

Drop the gnocchi into the boiling water. Stir gently to prevent sticking. When the gnocchi float to the top, they are cooked. Remove with a slotted spoon to a serving bowl.

Meanwhile, heat the sauce in a medium saucepan over medium heat. Top the gnocchi with the sauce.

KITCHEN TIP

Gnocchi will keep in the refrigerator for 1 to 2 days and for months in the freezer in an air-tight container.

WILD SALMON EN PAPILLOTE

Steaming fish in parchment is a wonderful way to seal in juices and create a spectacular presentation. In addition, the packages can be put together ahead of time and popped in the oven just before dinner. Always opt for unbleached parchment paper that's as chemical-free as possible.

1 cup basmati or white rice

1½ cups chicken broth or water

¼ cup chopped fresh mint

1 tablespoon olive oil

½ teaspoon salt

4 ounces soft goat cheese, such as chèvre

½ cup raisins

⅛ teaspoon freshly grated nutmeg

1½ tablespoons capers

4 wild salmon fillets (about 1 pound total)

Salt

Freshly ground black pepper

Juice of 1 orange

2 tablespoons finely chopped fresh chives

In a medium saucepan over high heat, bring the rice, broth or water, mint, oil, and salt to a boil. Reduce the heat to low, cover, and simmer for 20 minutes. Do not remove the lid. Remove from the heat and let stand, covered, for at least 10 minutes. Just before serving, fluff with a fork.

Meanwhile, preheat the oven to 450°F.

In a small bowl, combine the cheese, raisins, nutmeg, and capers.

Cut four 12-inch circles of parchment paper or foil. Rinse the salmon under cold water, pat dry, and place each on one half of the parchment or foil, about 1½ inches from the edge. Sprinkle each fillet with salt and pepper. Place one-quarter of the cheese mixture on top of each fillet. Sprinkle with one-quarter of the orange juice and the chives. Fold over the parchment and, starting at the edge of the half circle, using small folds, completely seal the fish and cheese mixture inside the parchment. Place the packets on a baking sheet and bake for 15 minutes. Remove from the oven and place a packet on each of 4 plates.

Tear through the parchment with a sharp-tipped knife. Put the remaining orange juice in a small saucepan over medium-high heat, reduce to about 3 tablespoons, and spoon over the cooked salmon. Serve with the rice.

FISH FILLET WITH PARSLEY-ALMOND PESTO

Any fish broiled with this lively pesto is transformed into a glorious meal. I like it with boiled potatoes and the first-of-the-season baby carrots. Drizzle a little extra cold pesto on the vegetables. The sauce tastes different when served chilled.

1 cup firmly packed curly parsley, stems removed

1 garlic clove

2 tablespoons slivered almonds

¼ cup grated Parmesan or Asiago cheese (about 1 ounce)

Juice of 1 large lemon

¼ cup extra-virgin olive oil (or enough to create a smooth, loose paste)

4 fresh or frozen fish fillets (about 1½ pounds total), such as Pacific halibut, Alaskan salmon, or Pacific sablefish

1 teaspoon paprika

Preheat the broiler. Lightly oil a broiler pan.

Combine the parsley, garlic, almonds, and cheese in a food processor or blender. Pulse until puréed. Add the lemon juice. With the machine running, gradually add the oil and purée until the sauce is smooth.

Brush both sides of the fillets with the pesto. Sprinkle with the paprika.

Place the fillets on the broiler pan and broil for 5 to 10 minutes, or until opaque.

VARIATIONS
I also like to serve this fish cold on top of a bed of salad greens, or pack it in a picnic basket along with a baguette for sandwiches in the park or on the beach.

GREEN GODDESS CHICKEN AND ASPARAGUS SALAD

At our catering company, we use this green goddess dressing throughout the spring and summer. It is especially good with asparagus, which is why this recipe is such a lovely way to combine fresh asparagus with leftover chicken.

½ cup chopped green onions

¼ cup chopped fresh Italian parsley

1 garlic clove

1 tablespoon fresh tarragon

1 tablespoon fresh dill

1 tablespoon red wine vinegar

½ cup sour cream or plain yogurt

½ cup buttermilk (see Organic Tip)

1½ teaspoons salt, plus extra for seasoning

1½ teaspoons sugar

¼ teaspoon freshly ground black pepper, plus extra for seasoning

1 pound asparagus

1 pound boneless, skinless chicken thighs or breasts, cut into bite-size pieces

Lettuce leaves for serving

4 whole spring onions, trimmed

In a food processor or blender, purée the green onions, parsley, garlic, tarragon, and dill. Add the vinegar, sour cream, buttermilk, salt, sugar, and pepper. Thin with water if necessary.

In a medium pot of boiling water, cook the asparagus for about 3 minutes, then remove with tongs or a slotted spoon and plunge in a bowl of ice water. Transfer to a large bowl.

Cook the chicken in the same water, drain, and plunge in the ice water to chill. Put in the bowl with the asparagus. Add enough dressing to coat generously, and toss the asparagus and chicken. Season with salt and pepper to taste.

Make a bed of lettuce leaves on a serving dish, mound with the asparagus and chicken, and garnish with whole spring onions.

ORGANIC TIP

Organic buttermilk is not as readily available as organic milk. In this recipe, you may substitute organic yogurt for the buttermilk. Be sure to ask your grocer to carry organic buttermilk. The more you ask, the more likely they are to see a need and start carrying it.

BEEF STEW WITH BABY SPRING VEGETABLES

MAKES
8
SERVINGS

Even in springtime, there are cool nights when a comforting stew can't be beat. When possible, keep the vegetables whole. If they are very large, cut them into large bite-size pieces.

1½ pounds beef stew meat

8 whole small shallots

2 tablespoons garam masala

1½ teaspoons salt

1 teaspoon freshly ground black pepper

8 cups assorted baby vegetables, such as carrots, beets, turnips, radishes, potatoes, and fennel (about 40 pieces)

6 garlic cloves, minced

2 celery ribs, finely chopped

4 sprigs fresh thyme

4 sprigs fresh Italian parsley

1 bay leaf

1 teaspoon ground cloves

2 teaspoons ground coriander

6 cups beef or chicken broth

Preheat the oven to 500°F.

Put the meat and shallots in a deep, large roasting pan. Sprinkle with the garam masala, ½ teaspoon of the salt, and ½ teaspoon of the pepper. Roast, turning the beef occasionally, for 30 minutes, or until browned.

Reduce the heat to 350°F.

Add the baby vegetables, garlic, celery, thyme, parsley, bay leaf, cloves, coriander, the remaining 1 teaspoon salt and ½ teaspoon pepper, and the broth. Stir to mix well.

Cover and roast, basting occasionally with the liquid, for 2½ to 3 hours, or until the meat is tender. Remove and discard the bay leaf and herb sprigs before serving.

LAMB BURGERS WITH CARAMELIZED SHALLOTS

When I am hungry for meat, there is nothing that compares with a great burger. Of course, you can use ground beef, turkey, chicken, pork, or even a good meat substitute instead of the lamb. It is the oniony flavor of these burgers, which comes from the caramelized shallots and bits of onion in the meat, that makes the difference for me.

1 tablespoon olive oil

8 ounces shallots, sliced

1 pound ground lamb

½ red onion, grated

1 garlic clove, minced

1 teaspoon finely chopped fresh rosemary

½ teaspoon salt

½ teaspoon freshly ground black pepper

4 whole wheat buns

Heat the oil in a large skillet over medium-high heat. Add the shallots and cook, stirring occasionally, for 7 minutes, or until soft and golden brown. Remove to a bowl.

Meanwhile, in a medium bowl, combine the lamb, onion, garlic, rosemary, salt, and pepper. Form into 4 burgers.

In the same skillet over medium heat, cook the burgers for 10 minutes, turning once, or until a thermometer inserted in the center registers 145°F for medium-rare.

Place the burgers on the buns and top with the shallots.

GORGONZOLA POTATOES AND PEAS

I am one of those people who skips dessert but over-indulges in creamy, rich dishes like this one. Even though potatoes and pasta may not sound impressive, this recipe is heavenly when tossed with egg noodles, and oh so decadent.

1½ pounds small red potatoes

1 pound fresh peas, shelled, or 1 cup frozen peas, thawed

4 tablespoons unsalted butter

¼ cup unbleached all-purpose flour

2 cups milk

4 ounces Gorgonzola cheese, crumbled

3 tablespoons chopped fresh chives

½ teaspoon freshly grated nutmeg

¼ teaspoon white pepper

Bring a large pot of salted water to a boil over medium-high heat. Cook the potatoes, whole and unpeeled, for 15 minutes, or until tender. Add the peas during the last 3 minutes of cooking time. Drain. Leaving the skin on the potatoes, cut into quarters.

Preheat the oven to 400°F, and lightly butter a 2-quart baking dish.

Melt the 4 tablespoons butter in a large saucepan over medium heat. Whisk in the flour and cook until the flour turns a light brown. Very gradually whisk in the milk. Simmer for 5 minutes, or until the sauce thickens. Stir in the cheese, chives, nutmeg, and pepper. Add the potatoes and peas and toss to coat well.

Pour into the prepared baking dish. Bake for 30 minutes, or until heated through and lightly browned.

ASPARAGUS RISOTTO
WITH TRUFFLE OIL

A little truffle oil goes a long way. If you can't find organic truffle oil, use a little more butter. This risotto is so simple and so delicious. It is wonderful on its own or as a side dish with grilled seafood.

4 cups vegetable or chicken broth

2 tablespoons olive oil

4 green onions or spring garlic, minced

1 cup Arborio rice

1 pound asparagus, trimmed and cut
    into 2-inch pieces

2 tablespoons unsalted butter

½ teaspoon freshly ground black
    pepper

1 tablespoon truffle oil

½ cup grated Parmesan cheese

Bring the broth to a boil in a medium saucepan over medium heat. Reduce the heat to low, cover, and maintain at a simmer.

Heat the oil in a heavy saucepan over medium heat. Add the green onions and rice and cook for 5 minutes, or until the rice is golden brown.

Begin adding the broth, ½ cup at a time, and cook, stirring constantly, for 20 minutes, or until all the broth is absorbed and the risotto becomes creamy. Just before adding the last ½ cup broth, add the asparagus, butter, and pepper.

Stir in the truffle oil and cheese and serve.

NOODLES WITH COTTAGE CHEESE, LEEKS, AND PEAS

MAKES
6
SERVINGS

I am an old-fashioned girl who still enjoys the pleasures of simple, uncomplicated dishes, which this recipe exemplifies. It is outstanding as an accompaniment for meat and poultry. But very often, I find myself eating only a few bites of meat and instead reaching for seconds of these wonderful noodles, enjoying them more as an entrée.

12 ounces egg noodles

1 pound fresh peas, shelled, or 1 cup frozen peas, thawed

1½ cups vegetable or chicken broth

2 pounds baby or small leeks, sliced (see Kitchen Tip)

1½ cups cottage cheese

2 tablespoons unsalted butter

2 tablespoons chopped fresh dill

2 tablespoons chopped fresh chives

Salt

Freshly ground black pepper

Cook the noodles according to package directions. Add the peas during the last 2 minutes of cooking.

Meanwhile, in a medium skillet over medium heat, bring the broth to a simmer and add the leeks. Reduce the heat to low, cover, and simmer for 5 to 7 minutes, or until the leeks are very soft. Remove with a slotted spoon and transfer to a large serving bowl. Reserve the broth.

Drain the noodles and peas and add to the bowl with the leeks. Add the cottage cheese, butter, dill, and chives. Stir until well blended and season with salt and pepper to taste.

If the noodles are not moist enough for your taste, add a few tablespoons of the reserved broth. Freeze remaining broth for future use.

KITCHEN TIP

Leeks are a dirty crop. A bit of the growing soil is usually found between the layers. The best way to clean leeks is to cut them in half lengthwise, and then crosswise into ½-inch slices. Soak in a large bowl of water for 5 minutes, stirring occasionally to dislodge the dirt, and letting it settle to the bottom of the bowl. Remove the leeks to a colander with a slotted spoon and rinse and drain.

SPRING ONIONS AMANDINE

Sometimes the simplest dishes are the most memorable. Spring onions are delicate, and this delicious way of serving them brings out their sweetness.

1 cup chicken or vegetable broth

1 pound spring onions with small bulbs or pearl onions

¼ teaspoon saffron threads (optional)

1½ tablespoons unsalted butter

½ cup whole almonds, coarsely chopped

1 tablespoon chopped fresh dill

¼ teaspoon salt

⅛ teaspoon freshly ground black pepper

In a medium saucepan over high heat, bring the broth, onions, and saffron (if using) to a boil. Reduce the heat to medium-low, cover, and simmer for 20 minutes, or until the onions are tender. Remove from the heat. Using a slotted spoon, remove the onions to a bowl and keep warm.

Return the pan to the heat and cook the liquid over high heat for 4 minutes, or until reduced to ¼ cup. Add the butter, almonds, dill, salt, and pepper and cook for 1 minute. Return the onions to the mixture and cook for 2 minutes longer, or until heated through.

KITCHEN TIP

For a richer version of this dish, after reducing the cooking liquid, add ¼ cup heavy cream.

WATERCRESS WITH STRAWBERRY VINAIGRETTE AND CHEDDAR CROUTONS

For this salad, it is best to use those overripe strawberries, the ones you consider throwing away because they are so soft and juicy. To make the purée, use a food processor or blender. Or, for a chunky strawberry vinaigrette, mash them with a fork.

Croutons

6 ounces smoked Cheddar cheese, or any smoked natural or local cheese

1 large egg

½ cup unbleached all-purpose flour

¾ teaspoon ground red pepper (cayenne, optional)

½ teaspoon salt

Salad

16 strawberries, hulled

3 tablespoons extra-virgin olive oil

3 tablespoons balsamic vinegar

1 garlic clove, minced

2 teaspoons chopped fresh thyme

½ teaspoon salt

¼ teaspoon freshly ground black pepper

8 cups watercress

1 avocado, halved, pitted, peeled, and sliced

1 green onion, finely chopped

To make the croutons: Preheat the oven to 350°F. Lightly oil a baking sheet.

Cut the cheese into ½-inch squares.

In a small bowl, beat the egg with 2 tablespoons cold water. In another small bowl, combine the flour, ground red pepper, if using, and salt. Working in batches, use your hands or tongs to toss the cheese in the flour. Then toss in the beaten egg and coat thoroughly. Toss again in the flour. Place on the prepared baking sheet. Bake for 15 minutes, or until lightly browned.

To make the salad: Meanwhile, put 12 of the strawberries in a food processor or blender and process until puréed. (You should have ½ cup.) Slice the remaining 4 strawberries and set aside.

In a large bowl, whisk together the strawberry purée, oil, vinegar, garlic, thyme, salt, and pepper. Add the watercress and toss to coat well.

Divide the watercress evenly among 6 plates. Arrange the avocado on the plates and top with the green onion, sliced strawberries, and croutons.

THE WORLD'S EASIEST VINAIGRETTE

6

SERVINGS

I have taught my boys that there are a handful of recipes they need to know in order to cook well and wow their friends. This basic vinaigrette is at the top of the list, along with piecrust, ricotta gnocchi, and homemade meat loaf.

2 garlic cloves, minced

¼ cup vinegar, such as balsamic, rice wine, raspberry, or sherry wine vinegar

½ teaspoon salt

¼ teaspoon freshly ground black pepper

½ cup extra-virgin olive oil

In a small bowl, combine the garlic, vinegar, salt, and pepper. Whisk in the oil until well blended.

VARIATIONS

Once you have the basic recipe, experiment with variations by adding different herbs, spices, or condiments. Here are a few of my favorite combinations.

Asian: Omit the salt; add 2 tablespoons soy sauce or tamari, 1 tablespoon grated fresh ginger, and 1 teaspoon toasted sesame oil.

Creamy blue: Add ¼ cup sour cream or plain yogurt and 4 ounces Gorgonzola or another blue cheese, crumbled.

Honey-mustard: Add 2 tablespoons honey and 1 tablespoon Dijon mustard.

HERB GARDEN
ANGEL FOOD CAKE

The roses and basil in the batter of this angel food cake create interest as well as a lovely flavor.

1 cup sifted cake flour

½ cup sifted confectioners' sugar

¼ teaspoon salt

1½ cups egg whites (about 12 large eggs), at room temperature

1½ teaspoons cream of tartar

1 teaspoon vanilla extract

1 cup granulated sugar

3 tablespoons chopped purple basil or regular basil

1 cup chopped organically grown rose petals

Preheat the oven to 350°F.

In a medium bowl, combine the flour, confectioners' sugar, and salt.

In a large bowl, beat the egg whites and cream of tartar with an electric mixer on high speed until frothy. Add the vanilla extract and beat until soft peaks form. Gradually beat in the granulated sugar, ¼ cup at a time, until glossy, stiff peaks form and the sugar dissolves. (To be sure that the sugar has dissolved, rub the beaten whites between your fingers. They should not feel granular.)

Gently fold the flour mixture into the egg white mixture in 4 stages. When the last bit of flour mixture is to be folded in, add the basil and rose petals.

Gently pour the batter into an ungreased 10-inch tube pan. Bake for 45 minutes, or until the top is golden brown and a wooden pick inserted in the center comes out clean.

Remove from the oven and invert the pan on a bottleneck, such as a wine bottle, and allow the cake to cool completely in the pan. When the cake is cool, run a thin knife between the cake and the pan. Turn out onto a plate.

KITCHEN TIP

For an extra-spectacular dessert, glaze the cake with a combination of 1 cup confectioners' sugar, 1 teaspoon pure vanilla extract, and 1 to 2 tablespoons milk. Add the milk gradually until the glaze has a spreadable consistency. Glaze the cake and garnish with additional organic rose petals.

BLACKBERRY SPICE CAKE

MAKES
8
SERVINGS

I find this cake somewhat whimsical—a simple spice cake studded with juicy blackberries. Serve it warm with vanilla ice cream or slightly sweetened whipped cream.

2 large eggs

⅓ cup vegetable oil

1 cup vanilla yogurt

1 cup packed brown sugar

1½ cups whole grain pastry flour

1½ teaspoons ground cinnamon

1 teaspoon ground ginger

1 teaspoon baking powder

¾ teaspoon ground allspice

½ teaspoon freshly grated nutmeg

½ teaspoon baking soda

½ teaspoon salt

1 pint blackberries

Preheat the oven to 350°F. Lightly oil a 9-inch cake pan.

In a medium bowl, combine the eggs, oil, and yogurt. Stir in the brown sugar.

In a large bowl, combine the flour, cinnamon, ginger, baking powder, allspice, nutmeg, baking soda, and salt. Form a well in the center and add the yogurt mixture, stirring just until blended. Fold in the blackberries.

Pour the batter into the prepared pan and bake for 50 to 55 minutes, or until a wooden pick inserted in the center comes out clean. Cool in the pan on a rack for 5 minutes. Run a knife around the inside of the pan and tap it on all sides to loosen the cake. Invert onto a serving plate.

KITCHEN TIP
You can substitute frozen berries for the fresh ones. Instead of mixing them into the batter, scatter them on the bottom of the pan before baking. When you invert the pan, the juices will act like a glaze.

74 SIMPLY ORGANIC

CHOCOLATE RICE PUDDING WITH RASPBERRY SAUCE

MAKES
10
SERVINGS

Rice pudding is one of my favorite desserts. It takes me back to the nights when my dad would make me a snack of milk and rice with a little sugar and vanilla. My love for rice pudding led me to this wonderful, rich, uncomplicated way of taking something humble and making it extraordinary. It's a great way to use up leftover rice.

2 cups half-and-half

4 ounces semisweet or bittersweet chocolate, chopped

1½ cups cooked rice

¾ cup plus 2 tablespoons sugar

1 teaspoon ground cinnamon

1 teaspoon vanilla extract

2 large eggs, beaten

1 cup raspberries

1 tablespoon balsamic vinegar

Preheat the oven to 350°F. Fill a large baking pan with 2 cups water. Have a 1½-quart baking dish ready, but do not grease it.

In a medium saucepan over medium heat, warm the half-and-half and chocolate, stirring constantly, for 3 minutes, or until the chocolate is melted. Remove from the heat.

In a medium bowl, combine the rice, ¾ cup of the sugar, the cinnamon, vanilla extract, and eggs. Whisk the half-and-half mixture into the rice mixture.

Pour into the baking dish and place the baking dish in the pan with the water. Bake for 50 to 60 minutes, or until a knife inserted in the center comes out clean.

Meanwhile, put the berries in a food processor or blender. Process until smooth. Transfer to a small bowl, add the remaining 2 tablespoons sugar and the vinegar and mash with a fork. Serve the sauce over the pudding.

SPRING CRÊPES WITH HONEY-MINT CRÈME FRAÎCHE

MAKES **5** TO **6** SERVINGS (10 TO 12 CRÊPES)

If it is early in the season and the fruit in your area is still on the tree or vine, use organic frozen, dried, or canned until fresh ripe food is available. With this approach, you can enjoy fruit-filled crêpes year-round. Sometimes I like to finish off crêpes with a dusting of confectioners' sugar, especially now that it is available in organic form.

4 large eggs

½ teaspoon salt

6 tablespoons sugar

1 cup unbleached all-purpose flour

½ cup milk

2 tablespoons unsalted butter, melted

1 cup crème fraîche or sour cream

2 to 3 tablespoons finely chopped fresh mint

2 tablespoons brown sugar

½ teaspoon vanilla extract

4 cups cut-up fresh fruit, such as cherries, apricots, or strawberries; or rehydrated dried fruit, such as cranberries, cherries, figs, peaches, or nectarines

Combine the eggs, ½ cup water, the salt, and 2 tablespoons of the sugar in a food processor or blender. Process until well blended. Gradually add the flour and milk and blend well. Add the melted butter and blend until smooth. Pour into a bowl, cover, and let sit at room temperature for 1 hour.

Meanwhile, in a small bowl, combine the crème fraîche or sour cream, mint, brown sugar, and vanilla. Refrigerate until ready to use. To make the crêpes, heat a well-seasoned skillet or a crêpe pan over medium-high heat. Pour a scant ¼ cup of the mixture into the pan, rolling it back and forth quickly in order to cover the surface thinly. Cook for 1 minute, or until the underside is brown, and invert onto a flat surface. Continue until all the crêpes are made. Just before serving, toss the cut-up fresh fruit with the remaining 4 tablespoons sugar. Mix and mash just a bit to release juices. (If you're using rehydrated fruit, taste and add the sugar only if needed.) Place about ⅓ cup of fruit on the uncooked side of each crêpe and fold into thirds to cover the filling. Serve with a dollop of the crème fraîche.

KITCHEN TIP
If you feel up to it, double the recipe for the crêpe batter, and freeze half of the crêpes, laying sheets of parchment paper between them.

MARIN SUN FARMS

It is more important than ever to choose our meat carefully, to know where it is grown and how it is processed. With the industrialization of the natural food industry, the reality of the terms *organic, pasture-raised, free-range, grass-fed, hormone-free,* and *antibiotic-free* must be questioned. There are many companies doing a great job right now, and it is up to you to examine their approach to animal husbandry and their use of growth hormones or antibiotics so you can decide which type of meat is best for you and your family.

Both small and large producers are adopting more sustainable practices as the demand for safe meat increases. Coleman Natural Meats is a great example of a larger company that offers beef, pork, lamb, and poultry that is completely natural. Niman Ranch has made a name for itself lately, producing pork and beef that is grown on small family farms throughout the United States.

The best choice is to buy locally and to support your neighborhood meat producer if you are fortunate to have one nearby. Marin Sun Farms is a meat producer close to my home and restaurants—a farm that, from start to finish, walks the walk when it comes to growing healthy animals and processing nourishing meat, while supporting the local environment and their community. Nestled in the rolling grasslands of the Point Reyes National Seashore in Northern California, Marin Sun Farms is committed to producing locally grown pasture-based food for the San Francisco Bay Area. To that end, they raise 100 percent grass-fed beef, lamb, goat, and pasture-raised chickens. Plus, they sell simply the best eggs you'll ever taste.

Owner David Evans is a staunch activist in the meat industry. He sees his farm, production, processing, and distribution as an effort toward a more sustainable food model. Marin Sun Farms is locally based, marketing its products within a 200-mile range. It supports its own community and economy by responsibly stewarding a sense of place by selling to nearby farmers' markets, restaurants, and grocers. Ultimately, the farm wants to have a connection to the people who buy and cook each juicy steak and succulent lamb shank. The ultimate result is a direct line from the ranch to the kitchen. They know their meat, poultry, and eggs end up nearby, on the tables of people who live close enough to visit the farm if they choose to. In essence, they are contributing to the overall health of the land, the water, the animals, and the people who enjoy the efforts of their ranching.

EARLY SUMMER

When the cooks in my kitchen at Flea St. Café start pleading for fresh tomatoes, I know summer has begun. After being deprived of sun-ripened tomatoes since mid-October, their patience has disappeared. Whether the early summer is warm or not, they want—even demand—tomatoes, symbols of the start of consistently warmer days. With the influence of Mediterranean cooking in our cuisine, tomatoes, as well as other summer vegetables, play important roles in our entrées. | But early summer is just that—early. The sun is just beginning to bathe heat-loving plants, such as tomatoes, in its warmth. It is a time of tiny but tasty foods. The tomatoes that we use during this season are cherry tomatoes, pint-size and delectably sweet. They make their way into salads, quick sauces, and sandwiches. | Mushrooms, herbs, potatoes, onions, squash blossoms, early eggplant, and peppers are also available. Stone fruits such as peaches, cherries, and apricots as well as blueberries and strawberries are in abundance and at their tastiest. We use fruits frequently in savory and sweet dishes. To support your organic kitchen, use this time to freeze as many fruits as possible for use later in the year. | My cooking takes its cue from the weather shifts common in early summer. As you will notice, this chapter offers quick, easy, and light recipes as well as those that take more time and warm up the kitchen. The real heat of summer is just around the corner.

SUMMER BEAN AND TOMATOES BRUSCHETTA

I like this appetizer because it is not only beautiful but also a light, fresh start to a meal. Both the beans and tomatoes need to be in small pieces to avoid too much mess. There are some great organic beers on the market, which I think are a perfect match for this dish.

1 cup miniature or cherry tomatoes, halved or quartered

½ small red onion, thinly sliced

1 garlic clove, minced

¼ cup thinly sliced fresh basil

3 tablespoons extra-virgin olive oil

2 tablespoons balsamic vinegar

½ teaspoon salt

2 ounces small green or wax beans, cut diagonally into ½-inch pieces

12 thick diagonal slices whole grain or hearty Italian bread

6 ounces soft goat cheese, such as chèvre

Freshly ground black pepper

Preheat the broiler. Bring a medium pot of water to a boil over high heat.

In a large bowl, combine the tomatoes, onion, garlic, basil, oil, vinegar, and salt. Toss to coat well. Let stand for at least 15 minutes.

Meanwhile, add the beans to the boiling water and cook for 3 minutes, or until tender-crisp. Drain and rinse with cold water. Add to the tomato mixture.

Place the bread slices on a broiler pan. Broil for 2 minutes, or until lightly browned on one side. Turn the slices and brush each with some of the juices from the marinated tomatoes. Broil for 2 minutes longer, or until browned.

Remove the bread and place on a large serving platter, moistened side up. Divide the cheese evenly among the bread slices and spread over each.

Scatter the tomato mixture over the cheese and sprinkle with pepper to taste.

EGGPLANT AND PARSLEY FRITTO MISTO

MAKES
4 TO 6
SERVINGS

Sometimes the simpler the food, the more intoxicating it can be. At Flea St. Café, we can never take the seasonal fritto misto off the menu. It is our customers' and staff's favorite way to eat fresh vegetables. We love it sprinkled with lots of salt, chased down with a martini or two. This recipe is for eggplant and Italian parsley, but any seasonal vegetable that cooks quickly can be substituted for the eggplant.

Vegetable oil for frying

2 cups buttermilk (see Organic Tip on page 38)

2 garlic cloves, minced

1 cup cornmeal

1 cup unbleached all-purpose flour

½ teaspoon ground red pepper (cayenne)

2 tablespoons chopped fresh thyme

Salt

Freshly ground black pepper

1 pound eggplant, such as globe, Rosa Bianca, or Japanese

Leaves of 1 small bunch Italian parsley

Heat 3 inches of oil in the bottom of a deep fryer or large stockpot until a deep-fat thermometer registers 350°F.

Meanwhile, in a medium bowl, combine the buttermilk and garlic.

In another bowl, combine the cornmeal, flour, ground red pepper, thyme, and salt and black pepper to taste.

Toss the eggplant in the buttermilk and then thoroughly coat with the flour mixture. Set aside until the oil is hot.

In small batches, fry the battered eggplant and add a few handfuls of the parsley leaves.

Drain on paper towels and salt generously. Repeat with remaining eggplant and parsley, making sure to maintain the temperature of the oil.

ROCK SHRIMP COCKTAIL WITH AVOCADO

Be sure to ask where the shrimp you purchase comes from and how it was harvested. Wild is fine when it is caught in a sustainable way. A lot of shellfish are being sustainably farm-raised, such as mussels, oysters, and shrimp. I like rock shrimp. Frozen or fresh, they are a good shrimp to use.

⅓ cup sour cream

2 tablespoons grated red onion

Salt

⅓ cup ketchup

2 heaping tablespoons grated
   horseradish

5 peppercorns, crushed with the side
   of a knife

1 bay leaf

12 ounces raw fresh or frozen rock
   shrimp, peeled

1 lime, halved

1 large avocado

1 teaspoon ground cumin

Freshly ground black pepper

In a small bowl, combine the sour cream, onion, and salt to taste. Cover and refrigerate. In another small bowl, combine the ketchup and horseradish. Cover and refrigerate.

Fill a large saucepan with water and add the peppercorns and bay leaf. Bring to a simmer over medium-high heat. Add the shrimp and cook for a few minutes or until they just begin to curl. Err on the side of undercooking for moister, more succulent shrimp.

Remove the shrimp with a slotted spoon and run under cold water to cool quickly. Set aside.

Juice half the lime in a small bowl. Cut the other half into wedges and set aside.

Halve and pit the avocado. Scoop the flesh into the bowl with the lime juice. Add the cumin and salt and pepper to taste. Mash with a fork.

Divide the avocado mixture evenly among 4 martini glasses or other attractive 8-ounce glasses. Top each one with one-quarter of the shrimp. Spoon a few tablespoons of the sour cream sauce on top. Finish with a spoonful of the horseradish sauce and a wedge of lime.

SMOKED CRAB CAKES

These tender crab cakes make a lovely first course. Serve large cakes over a bed of young salad greens tossed with vinaigrette for a sit-down course. Or, for a cocktail party, prepare smaller cakes and serve as finger food. Adding smoked seafood to crab cakes brings forth the natural sweetness of crab. When possible, use smoked wild seafood, which has become more available lately. Go for the dry, flaky smoked fish instead of the moist kind.

12 ounces lump crabmeat

4 ounces dry smoked fish, such as trout, whitefish, salmon, or halibut

½ cup mashed potato (white or sweet)

½ cup mayonnaise

1 tablespoon Dijon mustard

2 teaspoons Worcestershire sauce

3 green onions, thinly sliced

1 tablespoon chopped fresh dill

2 large eggs

½ cup unbleached all-purpose flour

Salt

Freshly ground black pepper

1 cup fresh bread crumbs

Vegetable oil for frying

In a large bowl, combine the crabmeat, smoked fish, potato, mayonnaise, mustard, Worcestershire sauce, green onions, and dill. Gently toss to blend. Form into 8 large or 16 small cakes.

Put the eggs in a small bowl and beat well.

Combine the flour and salt and pepper to taste in a pie plate or shallow bowl.

In another pie plate or shallow bowl, combine the bread crumbs with salt and pepper to taste.

Dip the crab cakes in the flour, then in the beaten egg, and finally coat well with the bread crumbs.

Heat ½ cup of oil in a large heavy skillet over medium-high heat. Working in batches, cook the crab cakes for 6 to 8 minutes, turning once, until browned. Add more oil to the skillet as needed. Remove to paper towels to drain.

SUMMER STRATA

If you can, use both zucchini and yellow squash in this wonderful, summery dish. Delicious as a first course, the strata is also a great addition to a brunch buffet and it makes a tasty light dinner. Challah or brioche are best here, but sweet Italian bread works, too.

2 tablespoons extra-virgin olive oil

2 medium zucchini or yellow squash, or 1 of each, thinly sliced

1 red onion, thinly sliced

2 garlic cloves, minced

12 large eggs

2 cups whole milk

½ cup chopped fresh basil

2 tablespoons chopped fresh oregano

1 cup unbleached all-purpose flour

¾ teaspoon salt

¼ teaspoon freshly ground black pepper

1 loaf challah, brioche, or sweet Italian bread (about 1 pound), torn into bite-size pieces

8 ounces soft goat cheese, such as chèvre or brie, broken into small pieces

⅓ cup sliced pitted green olives

½ cup grated Asiago or Parmesan cheese (about 2 ounces)

Preheat the oven to 350°F. Lightly oil a 13-by-9-inch baking dish.

Heat the olive oil in a large skillet over medium-high heat. Add the zucchini or yellow squash and onion and cook for 4 minutes, or until slightly softened. Remove from the heat and stir in the garlic. Drain off any liquid. Set aside to cool to room temperature.

In a large bowl, whisk together the eggs, milk, basil, and oregano. Gradually whisk in the flour, salt, and pepper.

Spread out the bread in the bottom of the prepared baking dish. Top with half of the zucchini mixture. Scatter half of the goat cheese and olives over the vegetables. Pour the egg mixture over all. Top with the remaining vegetables, goat cheese, and olives and press them gently into the egg mixture. Sprinkle with the grated cheese.

Bake for 45 minutes, or until a knife inserted in the center comes out clean. Let stand for 10 minutes before cutting. Serve warm or at room temperature.

VARIATIONS

Make this dish year-round, preferably with whatever is in season. Vary the cheese, as well. For the fall, try broccoli, cauliflower, and Cheddar. In the spring, use sliced snow peas and baby carrots with Swiss cheese.

HERB AND FLOWER–CRUSTED HALIBUT

4

SERVINGS

The herbs and blossoms coating this fish not only look spectacular, but also add a summery flavor to the light broth and peas beneath it. At Flea St. Café, we serve this over buttermilk-mashed potatoes, a heavenly mix.

½ cup chopped fresh Italian parsley

¼ cup chopped organically grown edible flower petals, such as calendula, nasturtiums, roses, or onion or chive blossoms

2 tablespoons chopped fresh chives

2 tablespoons chopped fresh basil

1 tablespoon chopped fresh oregano

½ teaspoon salt

¼ teaspoon freshly ground black pepper

1 halibut fillet (1½ pounds), cut into 4 pieces

2 tablespoons olive oil

1 cup chicken, vegetable, or fish broth

¼ teaspoon saffron threads

2 garlic cloves, minced

1 pound fresh peas, shelled, or 1 cup frozen peas, thawed

In a shallow bowl, combine the parsley, flower petals, chives, basil, oregano, salt, and pepper.

Place the halibut in the flower and herb mixture, pressing the fish to thoroughly coat both sides. Set aside.

Heat the oil in a large skillet over medium-high heat. Add the halibut and cook for 4 minutes on one side. Turn over the halibut and pour in the broth. Add the saffron and garlic. Simmer for 5 minutes, or until the halibut is just opaque and the broth is reduced by half. During the last minute or so, add the peas.

Remove the pan from the heat. Place 1 fish fillet in each of 4 shallow soup bowls. Divide the broth and peas evenly among the bowls.

VARIATION

Substitute salmon or any mild, firm fish fillet for the halibut. Whenever possible, try to buy line-caught, wild fish.

FRESH TUNA SALAD

This fresh tuna salad is far superior to the canned version. Use it in sandwiches, too.

1 lemon, halved

2 tablespoons chopped fresh dill, or 2 teaspoons dried

6 ounces tuna loin or steak

3 tablespoons extra-virgin olive oil

1 small onion, minced

2 celery ribs, or 1 small fennel bulb, chopped

1½ tablespoons capers

2 teaspoons Dijon mustard

2 tablespoons chopped fresh Italian parsley

2 teaspoons sugar

2 hard-cooked large eggs, peeled and chopped

Salt

Freshly ground black pepper

4 cups mesclun or another salad blend

1 avocado, halved, pitted, peeled, and sliced

Squeeze the juice from 1 lemon half into a medium bowl. Slice the other lemon half and place in a small skillet with 1 cup water and the dill. Bring to a boil over high heat. Add the tuna, reduce the heat to low, and simmer for 6 minutes, or until the tuna is opaque. Drain and chill thoroughly.

Meanwhile, to the bowl with the lemon juice, add the oil, onion, celery or fennel, capers, mustard, parsley, and sugar, whisking to blend the mixture well. Set aside.

When the tuna is cold, break it into bite-size pieces. Add the tuna and eggs to the bowl with the lemon juice mixture. Season with salt and pepper to taste and toss gently to coat the tuna.

Divide the mesclun evenly among 4 plates. Top each bed of mesclun with a quarter of the tuna salad. Fan a quarter of the avocado to the side of each tuna salad.

VARIATIONS

I love old-fashioned tuna melts. Mound lots of the tuna salad on a slice of bread, cover with a few slices of Jarlsberg or Cheddar cheese, and warm under the broiler.

When tomatoes are in season, add a few slices to tuna salads or sandwiches.

CHIPOTLE TURKEY MEATBALLS

I like to use ground dark turkey meat because it is moist and gives the meatballs more flavor than breast meat. You can find the dark meat in the poultry section of the meat case at large natural foods markets. Be sure to buy sustainably raised turkey. Heritage breeds of pasture-raised turkey are pricier, but well worth the cost, both because of their good flavor and the way the birds are treated.

½ cup ketchup

2 tablespoons honey

1 whole canned chipotle chile pepper, puréed or minced

1½ pounds ground dark turkey or chicken meat

1 medium onion, grated

2 medium carrots, peeled and grated

¼ cup chopped fresh Italian parsley

3 slices whole grain bread, torn into small pieces

1 teaspoon salt

¼ teaspoon freshly ground black pepper

½ cup chicken broth

1 large egg, beaten

Preheat the oven to 400°F. Generously oil a broiler pan or baking sheet with sides.

In a small bowl, combine the ketchup, honey, and chipotle. Set aside.

In a large bowl, combine the ground turkey, onion, carrots, parsley, bread, salt, and pepper.

In a small bowl, lightly beat the chicken broth and egg together and add to the meat mixture.

Mix well and form into 12 meatballs. Place the meatballs on the prepared pan. Spread a scant tablespoon of the ketchup mixture on each meatball.

Bake the meatballs for about 15 minutes, until well browned, or until a thermometer inserted in the center of a meatball registers 165°F.

ROASTED CHICKEN AND PEACHES

MAKES

6

SERVINGS

I prefer to roast a chicken whole. I think the meat stays moister, and I just like the way it looks when served. There are a growing number of organic chicken farms all over the country. I'm often asked what makes a chicken organic. The simple answer is that the chicken is fed only organic feed and is not injected with hormones or given unnecessary antibiotics.

1 teaspoon salt

½ teaspoon freshly ground black pepper

1 teaspoon ground cumin

1 whole chicken (about 3 pounds)

1½ teaspoons olive oil

4 leeks (white and light green parts),
    thinly sliced and washed thoroughly

6 peaches, pitted and quartered

3 tablespoons brown sugar

2 tablespoons chopped fresh tarragon

1 teaspoon ground cinnamon

½ teaspoon freshly grated nutmeg

Preheat the oven to 400°F.

In a small bowl, combine the salt, pepper, and cumin.

Rub the chicken with the oil and season generously with the cumin mixture. Place the chicken in a roasting pan.

In a large bowl, combine the leeks, peaches, brown sugar, tarragon, cinnamon, and nutmeg. Scatter the mixture around the bottom of the chicken in the pan.

Roast the chicken for 30 minutes. Stir the peaches occasionally to coat with the pan juices. Reduce the heat to 350°F and roast for 30 minutes more, or until a thermometer inserted in a breast registers 180°F and the juices run clear. Let stand for 10 minutes before carving.

Place the chicken on a platter, either whole or cut into pieces. Spoon the pan juices, leeks, and peaches over all.

STEAK WITH RASPBERRIES, FIGS, AND BLUE CHEESE

MAKES
8
SERVINGS

My dad had a grocery store, and my uncle owned the local meat-processing plant. They sold kosher natural meats. Although I didn't realize it at the time, the meat that my family ate was as close to organic as you could find in those days.

1 cup red raspberries

3 tablespoons sugar

2 tablespoons balsamic vinegar

1 tablespoon olive oil

1 small red onion, thinly sliced

8 large or 16 small figs, quartered

2 ounces ham, chopped

1 teaspoon finely chopped fresh rosemary

¾ teaspoon garam masala

Freshly ground black pepper

8 boneless rib-eye or beef tenderloin steaks (about 2½ pounds total)

Salt

6 ounces blue cheese, crumbled

Prepare a hot charcoal fire or preheat a gas grill on high, or preheat a broiler. Lightly oil the grill rack or broiler pan.

In a small saucepan over medium heat, combine the raspberries, sugar, and vinegar. Simmer for 10 minutes, or until reduced by half. Set aside.

Meanwhile, heat the oil in a medium skillet over medium heat. Add the onion and cook for 5 minutes, or until soft. Add the figs, ham, rosemary, garam masala, and ½ teaspoon of pepper. Cook for 5 minutes, or until the figs are very soft. Set aside and keep warm.

Season the steaks generously with salt and pepper. Grill or broil the steaks for 12 minutes, turning once, or until a thermometer inserted in the center registers 145°F for medium-rare.

Place each steak on a plate. Top with an equal amount of cheese and cover with some of the fig mixture. Drizzle a few tablespoons of the raspberry sauce over all. Serve the remaining fig mixture on the side.

ORGANIC TIP

These days, there are more options for finding well-raised cattle, which are freely grazed, free of growth hormones and antibiotics, and treated humanely. If you can find organic meat, always opt for it. I even buy frozen meat if it is organic. It's always worth the extra money. Natural meat is the second-best choice.

LAMB CHOPS WITH PEAS AND MATSUTAKE MUSHROOMS

There are a handful of organic lamb companies around the country, and the lamb they produce is wonderful. I like lamb chops on the bone. Those who don't pick them up with their fingers, enjoying every morsel, are missing out on the best part.

Matsutakes come from the Northwest—if you can't find them, shiitakes are a delicious substitute.

8 rib or loin lamb chops

5 tablespoons olive oil

3 garlic cloves, minced

2 tablespoons minced fresh rosemary

Salt

Freshly ground black pepper

3 medium shallots, thinly sliced

4 ounces fresh matsutake mushrooms, thinly sliced

¼ cup cream sherry

2 tablespoons chopped fresh marjoram or oregano

1½ pounds fresh peas, shelled (about 1½ cups)

Prepare a hot charcoal fire or preheat a gas grill on high, or preheat the broiler. Lightly oil the grill rack or broiler pan.

Put the lamb in a medium bowl and add 2 tablespoons of the olive oil, three-quarters of the garlic, and the rosemary, and season well with salt and pepper. Toss to coat the lamb. Let stand for 10 minutes.

Meanwhile, in a medium saucepan over medium heat, warm the remaining 3 tablespoons olive oil. Add the shallots and remaining garlic and cook for about 5 minutes, or until soft. Add the mushrooms, sherry, and marjoram or oregano and cook until the mushrooms begin to soften. Remove from the heat and set the saucepan aside.

Grill or broil the chops for 5 minutes, turning once, or until browned and a thermometer inserted in the center registers 145°F for medium-rare.

Just before serving, place the mushroom mixture over medium heat and add the peas. Cover the pan and cook for about 3 minutes, or until the peas are tender.

Divide the chops among 4 plates and top with the mushroom and peas.

PORT-BRAISED CIPOLLINI ONIONS

MAKES
4
SERVINGS

A few years ago, my dear friend Michael Romano, the chef at Union Square Cafe in New York City, took me to his home in the Hamptons. Rather than going out to eat as we always do when in the city, he cooked for me. We drank good wine and laughed and cried as friends sometimes do. But the most memorable part of the actual meal was his cipollini onions. This is my interpretation of his recipe.

1 cup ruby port

1 tablespoon chopped fresh thyme

1 cup vegetable or chicken broth

8 ounces cipollini onions or other small onions

2 tablespoons brown sugar

2 tablespoons unsalted butter

½ teaspoon salt

Pinch of red-pepper flakes (optional)

Combine the port, thyme, and ½ cup of the broth in a large skillet over high heat. Add the onions and bring to a boil. Reduce the heat to low, cover, and simmer for 30 minutes, or until the onions are very soft. Add the remaining ½ cup broth when all of the liquid evaporates.

When the onions are cooked, you should have ¼ cup reduced sauce. If you have more sauce, uncover and simmer over medium-high heat until reduced to ¼ cup. Add the brown sugar, butter, salt, and pepper flakes (if desired) and cook, uncovered, stirring occasionally, for 5 minutes.

KITCHEN TIP
Cipollini onions are ideal to cook alongside roasting meats or chicken. Add them at the very beginning; they impart flavor and also serve as a side dish.

94 SIMPLY ORGANIC

MOREL-STUFFED PATTYPAN SQUASH

MAKES

6

SERVINGS

Summer squash is an underrated vegetable. Because it is available year-round and is reasonably inexpensive and easy to prepare, it is not used when at its best: in late spring and early summer. These stuffed squash are a wonderful side dish for so many main courses, including fish and poultry. If you can't find fresh morels, substitute chanterelles or shiitakes.

6 medium pattypan squash

1½ cups vegetable or chicken broth

5 whole peppercorns

1 bay leaf

3 tablespoons olive oil

½ red onion, finely chopped

4 ounces morel mushrooms, sliced

1 garlic clove, minced

½ cup chopped fresh basil

1 tablespoon chopped fresh oregano

2 slices bread, torn into small pieces

1 large egg, beaten

4 ounces cream cheese, cut into small cubes

¼ cup grated Romano or Parmesan cheese (about 1 ounce)

Salt

Freshly ground black pepper

Preheat the oven to 375°F.

Put the squash in a large skillet and pour the broth over the squash. Add the peppercorns, bay leaf, and 1 tablespoon of the oil. Bring to a boil over high heat. Reduce the heat to low, cover, and simmer for 10 to 15 minutes, or until the squash are tender. Remove to a plate. Place a sieve over a medium bowl, strain the cooking liquid, and set aside.

Heat the remaining 2 tablespoons oil in a skillet over medium-high heat. Add the onion and cook for 5 minutes, or until soft. Add the mushrooms, garlic, basil, and oregano. Transfer to a large bowl. Add the bread, egg, cream cheese, grated cheese, and salt and pepper to taste. Moisten with ½ cup of the reserved cooking liquid.

When the squash are cool enough to handle, cut off the top quarter of each one. Using a spoon, remove and discard the seeds.

Place the squash in a baking pan. Fill the cavities of the squash with the mushroom mixture, mounding it on top of the squash, if necessary.

Pour the remaining cooking liquid into the pan. Bake for 20 minutes, or until heated through.

CUCUMBERS WITH CHILE AND DILL

MAKES
4
SERVINGS

You can start using cucumbers when they are very tiny and continue throughout the season. This lovely salad would be wonderful on a bed of heirloom oak leaf lettuce with a bit of the vinaigrette drizzled over all. I like to use lemon cucumbers, but any cucumbers will be delicious.

¼ cup seasoned rice vinegar

2 tablespoons extra-virgin olive oil

2 tablespoons chopped fresh dill

Salt

Freshly ground black pepper

1 large cucumber, very thinly sliced

1 red onion, thinly sliced

1 small hot chile pepper, thinly sliced

In a large bowl, whisk together the vinegar, oil, dill, and salt and black pepper to taste. Add the cucumber, onion, and chile pepper and let stand for at least 10 minutes.

KITCHEN TIPS

If you like, peel the cucumbers. For a less watery salad, seed the cucumbers by running the tip of a teaspoon down the center.

BLACK BEANS WITH CORN RELISH

This savory dish is like a bean stew. The corn relish is a wonderful way to showcase the first-of-the-season fresh corn, but it's equally good with frozen corn. Serve this with warm corn tortillas and top the beans and relish with a big dollop of sour cream.

Beans

2 tablespoons olive oil

1 onion, chopped

1 carrot, thinly sliced

1 celery rib, thinly sliced

2 garlic cloves, minced

⅓ cup chopped fresh jicama (½ small jicama)

3 cups cooked black beans (see Kitchen Tip)

8 ounces extra-firm tofu (regular or smoked), drained and cubed

1 cup vegetable broth

2 tablespoons chopped fresh oregano

1 teaspoon ground cumin

1½ teaspoons chili powder

1 teaspoon salt

Corn Relish

1½ cups fresh or frozen corn kernels

1 garlic clove, minced

2 green onions, thinly sliced

3 tablespoons chopped fresh basil

Juice of 1 lime

1½ teaspoons ground cumin

1½ tablespoons brown sugar

½ teaspoon salt

½ teaspoon red-pepper flakes or chopped chile pepper to taste

To make the beans: Heat the oil in a large skillet over medium heat. Add the onion, carrot, celery, garlic, and jicama and cook for 4 minutes, or until slightly softened. Add the beans, tofu, broth, oregano, cumin, chili powder, and salt. Bring to a boil. Reduce the heat to low, cover, and simmer, stirring occasionally, for 30 minutes.

To make the corn relish: Meanwhile, bring a small pot of water to a boil over high heat. Blanch the corn in the water for 3 minutes. Drain and immediately pour the corn into an ice bath to cool. Drain and put in a medium bowl. Add the garlic, green onions, basil, lime juice, cumin, brown sugar, salt, and red-pepper flakes or chile peppers.

To serve, divide the bean mixture evenly among 4 bowls and top with the corn relish.

KITCHEN TIP

To cook the beans, rinse 1 cup dried black beans and put in a large bowl with water to cover by 2 to 3 inches. Soak overnight and drain. Put the beans in a large saucepan and cover with water or chicken broth by about 2 inches. Simmer for about 1 hour, until tender.

FAVA BEANS AND ORZO SALAD

MAKES
4
SERVINGS

Fava beans, also known as "faba" or "broad beans," are very common in the Mediterranean.

4 ounces orzo or other small pasta

2 pounds fava beans in their pods

3 tablespoons extra-virgin olive oil

1 red onion, thinly sliced

2 garlic cloves, minced

1½ tablespoons chopped fresh
marjoram

3 tablespoons chopped oil-packed
sun-dried tomatoes

3 tablespoons red wine vinegar

Juice of 1 lemon

½ teaspoon salt

½ teaspoon freshly ground black pepper

1 bunch arugula (about 5 ounces)

Cook the orzo according to the package directions and drain.

Meanwhile, bring a large pot of water to a boil over high heat. Working in batches if necessary, boil the beans in their pods for 6 minutes, or until the beans inside are tender, but not mushy. Cool slightly. Remove and discard the pods. Using a small sharp knife, remove the outer skins of the beans.

Heat the oil in a large skillet over medium heat. Add the onion and garlic and cook for 7 minutes, or until very soft. Remove from the heat and stir in the marjoram, tomatoes, vinegar, lemon juice, salt, and pepper. Add the beans and orzo and toss to coat well.

Divide the arugula among 4 salad plates. Top with the bean salad.

KITCHEN TIP
You can substitute 3 cups fresh or frozen peas or lima beans for the fava beans.

SUMMER FRUIT SOUP

This refreshing and light dessert is welcomed by most, even after a big meal. It can be made with either fresh or frozen berries. When in season, float bite-size pieces of melon in the soup along with the berries. This soup is delicious served with crème fraîche or vanilla yogurt.

1 quart very ripe strawberries, hulled

3 cups orange juice

1 cup dry white wine

Grated zest of 1 lime

Juice of 2 limes

½ cup honey

2 tablespoons balsamic vinegar

2 tablespoons chopped fresh mint

3 whole black peppercorns

2 whole star anise

1 cinnamon stick

Salt

3 cups berries, such as raspberries, blueberries, or blackberries

In a large saucepan, combine the strawberries, orange juice, wine, lime zest, lime juice, honey, vinegar, mint, peppercorns, star anise, and cinnamon stick. Bring to a simmer over medium heat and cook for 15 minutes for the flavors to blend. Remove from the heat and cool to room temperature. Remove and discard the cinnamon stick and star anise. Season with salt to taste.

Place a food mill or ricer over a large bowl. Pour the soup through the mill and press into the bowl. Discard the seeds.

Chill the fruit broth. When ready to serve, ladle the broth into shallow bowls. Sprinkle generously with the uncooked berries.

KITCHEN TIP
Consider serving the soup as a warm dessert with ginger cookies.

EARLY SUMMER CHUTNEY

Chutney is relatively easy to make, and it keeps for weeks in the refrigerator. It is delicious served with roasted meats or poultry or as a spread on sandwiches. I particularly like it on a sandwich of smoked turkey and cream cheese.

2 cups sliced apricots (about 6 large)

2 cups pitted cherries, raspberries, strawberries, or blueberries

1 large onion, thinly sliced

2 cups packed brown sugar

1 cup cider vinegar

2 cinnamon sticks

¼ cup chopped fresh ginger

2 teaspoons salt

2 teaspoons red-pepper flakes (optional)

In a large saucepan, combine the apricots, cherries or berries, onion, brown sugar, vinegar, cinnamon sticks, ginger, salt, and red-pepper flakes, if using. Bring to a boil over medium-high heat. Reduce the heat to low and simmer, stirring occasionally, for 1½ hours, or until thickened. Remove from the heat and cool to room temperature. Remove and discard the cinnamon sticks.

Transfer the chutney to five 1-cup containers. Refrigerate for up to 1 month.

KITCHEN TIP

I love to share my chutney with my neighbors and friends. For a decorative presentation, wrap some fabric or twine around the jar. There is nothing that compares with a homemade gift from your kitchen.

BASIL-LEMON CAKE

Although a basil cake sounds unusual, think of the basil as you would mint, rather than as an herb used only in savory cooking. Mash cherries, berries, or any juicy sweet fruit and serve them over the cake with chocolate ice cream or whipped cream for an unbelievably luscious dessert.

2 cups unbleached all-purpose flour

½ cup coconut flour (see Kitchen Tips)

2½ teaspoons baking powder

½ teaspoon salt

½ cup (1 stick) unsalted butter, softened

1½ cups sugar

2 large eggs

½ cup chopped fresh basil

2 tablespoons finely grated lemon zest

1 teaspoon vanilla extract

1¾ cups buttermilk (see Organic Tip on page 38)

1½ cups mixed berries, such as raspberries and blackberries

Preheat the oven to 375°F. Lightly oil a 9-inch springform pan.

In a medium bowl, combine the flours, baking powder, and salt.

Combine the butter and sugar in a large bowl. With an electric mixer on medium speed, beat until creamy. Add the eggs, basil, lemon zest, and vanilla extract. Beat until blended.

Add the flour mixture, a third at a time, alternating with the buttermilk and beating on low speed until smooth.

Pour into the prepared pan. Bake for 35 to 45 minutes, or until a wooden pick inserted in the center comes out clean. Cool in the pan on a rack for 10 minutes. Remove the sides of the pan and cool completely.

Place the cake on a serving plate and top with the berries.

KITCHEN TIPS

This cake actually tastes better the next day. Cover well, but do not refrigerate unless you need to store it for more than 1 or 2 days.

If you can't find coconut flour, omit it, increase the all-purpose flour to 2½ cups, and reduce the buttermilk to 1 cup plus 2 tablespoons.

FRESH BERRY PIE

Use a variety of berries in this pie. My favorites are blackberries, raspberries, and blueberries. Strawberries are too juicy for this pie, so save them for another recipe. I like to make my pies in a 10-inch glass pie plate. It allows me to see the crust baking, and I love to hear people ooh and aah over a big old beautiful pie.

Crust

½ cup whole grain pastry flour

½ cup whole wheat flour

1 teaspoon ground cinnamon

1 teaspoon sugar

¼ teaspoon salt

½ cup (1 stick) cold unsalted butter

½ cup ice water

Filling

3 pints fresh berries, such as blackberries, raspberries, and/or blueberries, or 18 ounces partially thawed frozen berries, drained well

1¼ cups sugar

3 tablespoons tapioca

Grated zest of 1 lemon

1 tablespoon fresh lemon juice

Preheat the oven to 350°F.

To make the crust: In a large bowl, combine the pastry flour, whole wheat flour, cinnamon, sugar, and salt. Grate the butter into the flour mixture. Using your hands or a pastry blender, work the butter into the flour mixture until the pieces are about the size of peas. Add the water, 1 tablespoon at a time, and blend until a soft, moist dough forms.

Shape the dough into a flat, round disk. Wrap in plastic wrap and refrigerate for at least 1 hour.

To make the filling: When the dough has chilled, in a medium bowl, combine the berries, sugar, tapioca, lemon zest, and lemon juice. Toss to coat the berries well.

Place the dough on a well-floured surface and roll to about ⅛-inch thickness, turning over the dough often to keep it well floured. Fold the dough in half and place in a 9- or 10-inch pie plate. Unfold the dough, turn under the edges, and crimp them. Spoon the berry filling into the crust.

Bake for 1 hour, or until the crust is lightly browned. Place on a rack to cool for at least 30 minutes before slicing.

KITCHEN TIP

Most people like ice cream or whipped cream on their pie, but because of the sweetness of this filling, I prefer a big dollop of sour cream.

FRONTIER NATURAL PRODUCTS CO-OP

For years our restaurant kitchens have been buying dried organic herbs and spices in bulk from the Frontier co-op. It is one of the pioneers in the organic food movement, and has maintained its integrity throughout a thirty-year period of phenomenal growth.

It all began in 1976 in a simple cabin along the Cedar River in eastern Iowa, where two people passionate about organic and natural products formed a company called Frontier Natural Products Co-op. More than thirty years later, Frontier has grown from a small startup into one of the world's largest suppliers of organic herbs and spices. Its three brands—Frontier, Simply Organic, and Aura Cacia—can be found in natural foods and grocery stores across the United States and Canada.

Frontier's founders built their business on the belief that food should be grown on land that has been free from the use of synthetic fertilizers, growth regulators, insecticides, and herbicides. The company remains a champion of organic and sustainable agriculture. Its employees believe that fostering environmental responsibility is crucial to the world's future.

"We want to encourage growing and processing that helps protect, rather than deplete, our natural resources," says Tony Bedard, CEO of Frontier. "We visit growers all over the world to make sure our suppliers practice sustainable farming and respect the environment."

In 1988, Frontier introduced its first line of packaged spices. The line sold well and eventually led to the establishment of the Simply Organic brand, which appeared in 2002.

Simply Organic is an all-organic brand that offers spices, spice blends, and seasoning mixes for items like sauces, chili, dips, and dressing mixes. Simply Organic has quickly become the leading brand in the organic seasonings category.

Frontier's most sustained and dramatic success with product expansion has been in the area of aromatherapy. In its early days, the company bought bulk quantities of essential oils and rebottled them into one-half-ounce glass bottles. This line expanded as aromatherapy became increasingly popular.

In 1993 Frontier purchased Aura Cacia, an aromatherapy and natural personal care products company. In the years since, Aura Cacia has become a leading seller in natural health outlets nationwide. Products include essential oils, massage and body oils, mineral baths, and lotions.

As the largest supplier of organic herbs and spices, Frontier recognizes its responsibility to help convert food producers to sustainable farming and production practices.

Frontier gives back 1 percent of sales of Simply Organic's spice brand to the support of organic farming causes. The company also recently initiated a Sustainable Sourcing program that goes beyond the scope of the USDA's Fair Trade program. It establishes guidelines for suppliers to ensure ethical business conduct and sustainable farming practices.

As consumers increasingly look for products that represent sound social and environmental values, Frontier is looking forward to many more years of success in the future.

MIDSUMMER

Ah, summertime, and the cookin' is easy. I find myself wanting to make salads and dishes that don't require a lot of stove time. The outdoor grill gets more attention as I enjoy roasting and grilling fresh vegetables for pastas, salads, and appetizers. | Everywhere, gardens have hit their stride. This is the opposite of deep winter: So many varieties of fruits and vegetables are in abundance. I celebrate this bounty. I also remind myself not to let the sheer volume stop me from appreciating and enjoying the pleasure that each fruit and vegetable offers. | A visit to a farmers' market in midsummer can make me feel like a kid in a candy shop. At times, the selection in summer is almost too enticing, even for me. All too often, as I unpack my overflowing basket at home, I wonder what I was thinking and how I will have the time to prepare everything. Then I motivate myself to prepare as much as possible for easy use during the week ahead. | For example, I pull out my trusty steamer and steam as many fresh items from my basket as possible. I remind myself that this hour or two that I spend on a weekend will reward me with quickly assembled meals during the week. My refrigerator is stocked with organic vegetables, fruits, salads, and even steamed fish. They can be eaten as is or with a little seasoning. I also add them to pastas, grains, meats, and poultry; use them as side dishes; and toss them in a vinaigrette.

CHILLED TOMATO SOUP

MAKES 4 TO 6 SERVINGS

This recipe shows up more often than any other at our summertime catering gigs. We like to garnish it with freshly fried corn tortilla chips, and bamboo skewers of avocado. It is a great way to use tomatoes at any point in the season. If the tomatoes don't have much flavor, use a little sugar to enhance it. In winter, if you are craving tomato soup, use canned organic ones. Picked at their prime, they will offer better flavor and nutrition than fresh tomatoes shipped from the far reaches of the world.

3 pounds very ripe, juicy tomatoes (any color), coarsely chopped

1 medium red onion, coarsely chopped

1 cup firmly packed fresh basil

¼ cup olive oil

Juice of ½ lemon

1 teaspoon ground cumin

1 teaspoon ground turmeric

Salt

Freshly ground black pepper

Sugar (optional)

Working in batches if necessary, purée the tomatoes, red onion, and basil in a food processor or blender until smooth. Remove to a large bowl. For a more refined soup, push through a medium food mill or sieve to remove the skin, seeds, and coarse pulp.

Add the olive oil, lemon juice, cumin, and turmeric, and season with salt and pepper to taste. Add sugar if needed. Chill until ready to serve.

FRESH CORN BITES
WITH TARRAGON

MAKES ABOUT
18
BITES

If you are looking for a way to use up leftover steamed or grilled corn, this is it. These delicious bites are a hit at most of our catering functions.

2 cups cooked corn kernels
(2 to 3 medium ears of corn)

2 large eggs, beaten

3 tablespoons unbleached all-purpose flour

2 tablespoons chopped fresh tarragon

¾ teaspoon sweet paprika

⅛ scant teaspoon nutmeg

Salt

Freshly ground black pepper

1 cup heavy cream

Preheat the oven to 375°F. Lightly oil 18 mini-muffin cups (1 or 2 pans).

Put the corn in a medium bowl and, using a fork, mash to bring out the juices and pulp. Alternately, put the corn in a food processor, process, and transfer to a bowl.

Stir in the eggs, flour, tarragon, paprika, and nutmeg and season generously with salt and pepper. Whisk in the heavy cream and continue whisking until well blended.

Place the muffin pan in a jelly-roll pan and place in the oven. Pour about 1½ cups water into the jelly-roll pan. Bake the muffins for about 10 minutes or until they are puffed and rounded and a wooden pick inserted in the center comes out clean.

GARLIC BREAD WITH ROASTED SWEET PEPPERS

MAKES
10
SERVINGS

Use peppers when they are at their peak and in abundance. Lots of new varieties can be found at farmers' markets and ethnic grocery stores. They make a nice change from the usual red bell peppers in every grocery store. If you prefer, roast the peppers over an open flame, such as a gas burner, and then remove the skin. I like to roast peppers in the oven; it works just as well and takes half the effort.

1 pound sweet bell peppers, such as red, yellow, orange, or purple

2 tablespoons balsamic vinegar

1 tablespoon extra-virgin olive oil

2 tablespoons chopped fresh chives

2 tablespoons chopped fresh sage or basil

¼ teaspoon salt

¼ teaspoon freshly ground black pepper

4 tablespoons unsalted butter, softened

3 garlic cloves, minced

¾ teaspoon paprika

1 medium loaf Italian bread

1 cup grated Parmesan, Romano, or a similar aged grating cheese

Preheat the oven to 400°F.

Spread out the peppers on a baking sheet. Bake for 15 minutes. When they are slightly blackened and the skin is blistering on one side, turn them and cook for 15 minutes longer. Remove from the oven but do not turn off the oven. Put the peppers in a large bowl. Cover with a plate to steam. Let cool for 15 minutes.

Peel off and discard the skins, and remove and discard the seeds and stems. Slice or tear the peppers into thin strips. Return to the bowl. Add the vinegar, oil, chives, sage or basil, salt, and pepper. Toss to coat well. Set aside.

In a small bowl, combine the butter, garlic, and paprika. Slice the bread in half lengthwise.

If the bread is thick, remove some of the inside, leaving a hollow shell. Place the bread halves, cut side up, on a baking sheet. Spread thinly with the garlic butter. Sprinkle with the cheese. Bake for 15 minutes, or until lightly browned.

Place the bottom bread half on a cutting board. Arrange the roasted peppers on top. Cover with the other bread half. Press lightly. Cut crosswise into 10 slices.

VARIATIONS

If you want to add spice to the dish, add a fresh chile pepper or two when you roast the bell peppers.

To make this dish more substantial for a great lunch entrée, place slices of meat or chicken on top of the roasted peppers.

ZESTY ZUCCHINI QUESADILLAS

MAKES
4
SERVINGS

A favorite and easy snack in my home, these quesadillas are the perfect way to use abundant zucchini and tomatoes. Serve as a light lunch along with a tossed salad.

2 tablespoons pine nuts

2 tablespoons olive oil

1 zucchini, shredded

½ red or yellow bell pepper, finely chopped

1 small red onion, thinly sliced

2 garlic cloves, minced

1 teaspoon ground cumin

¼ cup chopped fresh cilantro

¼ teaspoon salt

¼ teaspoon freshly ground black pepper

1 large tomato, seeded and chopped

Juice of 1 lime

1 teaspoon chili powder

¼ teaspoon hot-pepper sauce (optional)

4 whole wheat or white flour tortillas (8 inches in diameter)

2 cups shredded Monterey Jack cheese (about 8 ounces)

Toast the pine nuts in a heavy-bottomed sauté pan over medium-high heat, stirring often, until they turn a golden brown. Cool.

Heat the oil in a medium skillet over medium heat. Add the zucchini, bell pepper, onion, garlic, and cumin. Cook for 5 minutes, or until all the vegetables are soft. Stir in the cilantro, salt, and black pepper. Set aside.

In a small bowl, combine the tomato, lime juice, chili powder, and hot-pepper sauce, if using.

Spread one-fourth of the zucchini mixture evenly over half of each tortilla. Sprinkle each with 1½ teaspoons pine nuts and one-fourth of the cheese. Fold the tortillas in half.

In a large skillet over medium-low heat, cook the quesadillas for about 5 minutes, turning once, until the cheese is melted.

Cut the quesadillas into wedges and top with a generous amount of the tomato mixture.

GREEK SALAD SANDWICHES

There is little that compares with just-harvested shelling beans. When cooked, mashed with a little feta cheese and olive oil, and then warmed inside a pita pocket, they are heavenly. These sandwiches, accompanied by the simple tomato-cucumber salad, make a healthy meal with a wonderful range of Mediterranean flavors.

2 cups freshly shelled beans, such as fava, lima, or cranberry

1 garlic clove, minced

1 tablespoon chopped fresh oregano

4½ tablespoons extra-virgin olive oil, plus extra as needed

6 ounces feta cheese, crumbled

Salt

Freshly ground black pepper

1 cucumber, peeled, halved, and thinly sliced

½ small red onion, thinly sliced

1 large tomato, seeded and chopped

2 tablespoons chopped fresh mint

2 tablespoons chopped fresh Italian parsley

Juice of 1 lemon

6 large whole wheat pitas (8 inches in diameter)

Preheat the oven to 375°F.

Bring 1 cup water to a boil in a small saucepan over medium heat. Add the beans. Simmer for 10 to 15 minutes, or until soft. Transfer the beans and cooking liquid to a medium bowl and mash with a potato masher or fork. Add the garlic, oregano, and about 3 tablespoons of the oil, or enough to give the beans the texture of a smooth pâté. Stir in the cheese. Season with salt and pepper to taste and set aside.

In a medium serving bowl, combine the cucumber, onion, tomato, mint, parsley, lemon juice, and the remaining 1½ tablespoons oil. Season with salt and pepper to taste.

Cut the pitas in half and open to form pockets. Spread an equal amount of the bean mixture

in each pita pocket. Gently press together. Place on a baking sheet and cover with foil. Bake for 10 minutes, or until warmed. Remove from the oven and cut into halves or quarters.

Place the cucumber salad in the middle of a large platter. Surround with the bean sandwiches.

KITCHEN TIP

If you don't grow shelling beans and can't find them at your grocery store, buy one of the excellent canned whole organic beans on the market. Simply mash the rinsed and drained beans with a bit of the canning liquid until they are the consistency of hummus.

VEGETABLE STEW WITH POLENTA

MAKES

6

SERVINGS

Like most stews, this one is even better the next day, after the flavors have had time to marry. Use any summer vegetables you choose. Begin by cooking the ones that take the longest and finish with the ones that need barely any cooking, like corn, peas, or beans.

Polenta

1 cup polenta

½ cup grated Asiago or Parmesan
    cheese (about 2 ounces)

1 tablespoon chopped fresh rosemary

Stew

2 tablespoons olive oil

2 garlic cloves, minced

1 onion, chopped

8 ounces shiitake mushrooms,
    stemmed and sliced

1 large tomato, peeled, seeded, and
    coarsely chopped

1 large carrot, sliced

1 small fennel bulb or 2 celery ribs, sliced

2 potatoes, cubed

3 cups vegetable or chicken broth

5 whole black peppercorns

1 bay leaf

8 large sprigs fresh herbs, such as dill,
    oregano, basil, marjoram, or sage,
    or a combination

3 tablespoons light miso or soy sauce

⅔ cup fresh or frozen peas

1 cup fresh or frozen corn kernels

Chopped fresh Italian parsley for
    garnish

To make the polenta: Lightly oil a 9-inch square baking dish.

Bring 4 cups water to a boil in a medium saucepan over medium heat. Gradually add the polenta, whisking constantly. Cook, whisking often, for 30 minutes, or until the polenta thickens and is creamy. Stir in the cheese and rosemary.

Pour the polenta into the prepared baking dish. Smooth the top and refrigerate for 30 minutes, or until firm.

To make the stew: Meanwhile, heat the oil in a large stockpot over medium heat. Add the garlic, onion, mushrooms, tomato, carrot, fennel or celery, and potatoes and cook, stirring occasionally,

for 10 minutes. Add the broth, peppercorns, bay leaf, and herb sprigs.

In a small bowl, blend the miso or soy sauce with 2 tablespoons water until smooth. Add to the stockpot.

Bring to a boil over medium-high heat. Reduce the heat to low and simmer for 1½ hours, or until the flavors are well blended. Stir in the peas and corn.

Just before serving the stew, remove the polenta from the refrigerator and cut into 1-inch squares. Remove and discard the bay leaf and herb sprigs from the stew. Place 4 to 5 polenta squares in the bottom of each of 6 soup bowls and ladle the stew over the top. Garnish with the parsley.

116 SIMPLY ORGANIC

SALMON SALAD WITH RASPBERRY VINAIGRETTE

Warm chunks of salmon are delicious on a bed of zesty arugula. The raspberry vinaigrette adds a sweetness that mellows out this dish perfectly.

1 cup raspberries

¼ cup extra-virgin olive oil

3 tablespoons balsamic vinegar

2 tablespoons brown sugar

4 sprigs fresh tarragon, finely chopped

1 garlic clove, minced

½ teaspoon salt

½ teaspoon freshly ground black pepper

¾ cup whole wheat flour

2 tablespoons finely chopped fresh chives

1 salmon fillet (about 12 ounces), skinned and cut into 4 pieces

1 large bunch (about 6 ounces) arugula, torn into bite-size pieces

1 large yellow or red tomato, cut into wedges

In a small bowl, mash the raspberries with a fork. Place a food mill or sieve over a medium saucepan and push the raspberries through, discarding the seeds. Add 2 tablespoons of the oil, the vinegar, sugar, tarragon, garlic, ¼ teaspoon of the salt, and ¼ teaspoon of the pepper. Place over low heat and bring to a simmer.

Meanwhile, in a pie plate, combine the flour, chives, and the remaining ¼ teaspoon each of salt and pepper. Coat the salmon with the flour mixture.

Heat the remaining 2 tablespoons oil in a medium skillet over medium-high heat. Add the salmon and cook for 7 to 8 minutes, turning once, or until just opaque.

Put the arugula and tomato in a serving bowl and toss with the warm vinaigrette. Break the salmon fillets into large pieces and place on top of the arugula.

SAVORY MUSSEL STEW

The beauty and integrity of this dish come from the ingredients. Though it is a summer dish, it can also be wonderful on a cold winter's night—just substitute canned organic tomatoes for the fresh. Whether it's summer or winter, be sure to serve with a loaf of dense, crusty bread to dip into this lovely broth.

2 tablespoons extra-virgin olive oil

2 large shallots, chopped

8 ounces andouille sausage or a similar spicy smoked sausage, cut into ¼-inch pieces

4 garlic cloves, chopped

½ cup dry white wine

4 large tomatoes, peeled, seeded, and chopped

1 cup firmly packed fresh basil, thinly sliced

2 tablespoons chopped fresh marjoram or oregano

1 teaspoon paprika

½ teaspoon freshly ground black pepper

2 cups clam juice

3 pounds mussels, scrubbed and beards removed

½ cup grated Romano cheese (about 2 ounces)

Warm the oil in a large saucepan over medium heat. Add the shallots and sausage. Cook for 3 minutes. Stir in the garlic and wine and cook for 1 minute longer. Add the tomatoes, basil, marjoram or oregano, paprika, and pepper. Cook, stirring, for 2 minutes.

Add the clam juice, increase the heat to high, and bring to a boil. Reduce the heat to low and add the mussels. Cover and simmer for 8 minutes, or until the mussels open. Discard any unopened mussels. Taste and adjust the seasoning.

Serve with the cheese.

KITCHEN TIP

For a more refined and elegant dish, after completing the recipe, remove the mussels and dislodge the meat, discarding the shells. Add ½ cup heavy cream to the stew and cook for 3 minutes over high heat. Return the mussels to the pan and mix thoroughly. Taste and adjust the seasoning.

PANCETTA AND LEEK-STUFFED PORK CHOPS

This moist, smoky stuffing adds exquisite flavor to the pork chops. Delicious pork from heritage breeds of pigs is available in most natural foods markets. Be sure to pay a little more instead of supporting the unethical confinement methods used to raise pigs for inexpensive, high-volume pork products.

2 ounces pancetta or guanciale (cured pig cheek)

2 large leeks, cut into ¼-inch rounds and cleaned thoroughly

3 garlic cloves, minced

1 tablespoon chopped fresh sage

Salt

Freshly ground black pepper

4 pork chops, 1 inch thick (bone-in or boneless)

2 tablespoons olive oil

2 tablespoons chopped fresh ginger

Prepare a hot charcoal fire or preheat a gas grill on high, or preheat the broiler. Lightly oil the grill rack or broiler pan.

Cut the pancetta into ¼-inch dice. In a medium skillet, over medium heat, cook for 4 minutes or until the fat is rendered and the pancetta is browned. Add the leeks and garlic and cook until very soft. Add the sage and season with salt and pepper to taste.

Cut a slit in the middle of each pork chop, creating a pocket. Fill each pocket with one-fourth of the leek filling.

In a small bowl, combine the olive oil, ginger, and salt and pepper to taste. Brush the mixture on the pork chops.

Place the chops on the grill rack or broiler pan, 4 inches from the heat source, and grill for 14 minutes, turning once, or until the juices run clear and a thermometer inserted in the meat reaches 145°F.

DEEP-DISH SUMMER VEGETABLE COBBLER

There are so many choices of vegetables to cook with at this time of the year. Use what you like, but make sure each is cooked until tender before adding it to the sauce.

Crust

1½ cups unbleached all-purpose flour

¼ cup whole wheat flour or cornmeal

2½ teaspoons baking powder

½ teaspoon salt

¼ teaspoon ground red pepper (cayenne)

½ cup finely chopped fresh Italian parsley

4 tablespoons cold unsalted butter, grated

1 cup shredded Cheddar cheese (about 4 ounces)

1 cup buttermilk (see Organic Tip on page 38)

Filling

4 tablespoons unsalted butter

1 large shallot, minced

3 tablespoons unbleached all-purpose flour

2 cups milk or vegetable broth

¼ cup Madeira wine (optional)

2 tablespoons chopped fresh sage

3 cups cooked vegetables, such as zucchini, eggplant, fennel, and bell peppers, cut into bite-size pieces

½ teaspoon salt

¼ teaspoon freshly ground black pepper

1 cup shredded Cheddar cheese (about 4 ounces)

To make the crust: In a large bowl, combine the all-purpose flour, whole wheat flour or cornmeal, baking powder, salt, ground red pepper, and parsley. Add the butter and cheese and stir in the buttermilk just until blended. Refrigerate while you make the filling.

To make the filling: Preheat the oven to 375°F. Lightly oil a 3-quart baking dish.

Melt the butter in a medium saucepan over medium heat. Add the shallot and whisk in the flour. Cook, stirring constantly, for 3 minutes, or until the mixture turns golden brown. Slowly whisk in the milk or broth and wine, if using. Whisk until slightly thickened. Add the sage, vegetables, salt, and pepper.

Transfer the creamed vegetables to the prepared baking dish. Sprinkle with the cheese. Drop the crust mixture by the tablespoon on top of the vegetables. Bake for 20 minutes, or until the crust is browned. Remove from the oven and let stand for 10 minutes before serving.

VEGETABLE RISOTTO WITH GOAT CHEESE

There is nothing as comforting and delicious as a bowl of creamy risotto. During the summer months, taking advantage of fresh vegetables makes this dish a seasonal delight.

4 cups chicken or vegetable broth

2 tablespoons olive oil

1 fennel bulb, thinly sliced

2 garlic cloves, minced

1 cup Arborio rice

4 ounces soft goat cheese, such as chèvre

1 cup fresh or frozen peas, thawed

1 tomato, seeded and chopped

2 tablespoons chopped fresh mint or basil

Bring the broth to a boil in a large saucepan over medium heat. Reduce the heat to low, cover, and maintain at a simmer.

Heat the oil in a deep, heavy saucepan over medium heat. Add the fennel, garlic, and rice. Cook for 5 minutes, or until the rice is golden brown. Begin adding the simmering broth, ½ cup at a time, and cook, stirring constantly, for about 20 minutes. Use enough of the broth for the risotto to become creamy. When done, the rice should still be a little firm in the center.

Stir in the cheese, peas, tomato, and mint or basil. Cook for 2 minutes and serve.

GRILLED GREEN TOMATOES

The first time I ever ate green tomatoes was my Dad's way, straight off the barbecue, smoky and succulent. Dad had an organic garden, and his tomatoes were its prize. We ate green tomatoes at both the beginning and the end of the growing season. Although I also love the crusty fried version, to this day, my favorite green tomatoes come hot off the grill.

4 large green tomatoes, cut into ½-inch-thick slices

¼ cup extra-virgin olive oil

2 garlic cloves, minced

1 tablespoon chopped fresh oregano

Salt

Freshly ground black pepper

Prepare a hot charcoal fire or preheat a gas grill on high. Lightly oil the grill rack.

Put the tomatoes in a large bowl. Add the oil, garlic, and oregano. Toss the tomatoes to thoroughly coat. Season generously with salt and pepper. Place the tomatoes on the grill and cook each side for 3 to 5 minutes, or until the tomatoes are tender.

KITCHEN TIPS

This is a perfect way to use those tomatoes that never quite ripened. If you pick green tomatoes when they are very firm, they will keep in the vegetable bin of your refrigerator for a few weeks.

While the grill is hot, make extra tomatoes and refrigerate them for later use. They're great in scrambled eggs, on sandwiches, or as a side dish for grilled meats or poultry.

SUMMER SUCCOTASH

Just-picked corn and beans barely need to be cooked. Tossed together with sweet red peppers and tomatoes, they are so good that I can't seem to get enough. This light dish should be eaten with a spoon, so you can savor all the flavors in each and every bite.

4 ounces green beans, cut into ½-inch pieces

2 ears corn, kernels removed

½ ripe red bell pepper, seeded and chopped coarsely

2 green onions, thinly sliced

1 tomato, seeded and coarsely chopped

1 jalapeño chile pepper, finely chopped

½ cup finely chopped fresh basil

½ teaspoon ground cumin

1 teaspoon sugar

Juice of 1 large lime

Salt

Freshly ground black pepper

About 2 tablespoons chopped fresh Italian parsley

Fill a medium saucepan two-thirds full with water. Place over high heat and bring to a boil. Add the beans and corn kernels. Cook for 3 minutes, or until tender-crisp. Drain and transfer to a large bowl.

Add the bell pepper, green onions, tomato, chile pepper, basil, cumin, sugar, and lime juice.

Season with salt and black pepper to taste. Sprinkle with parsley and toss to coat well.

KITCHEN TIP
On a warm summer night, serve this dish with chilled seafood or a grilled lamb or pork chop to complete the meal.

SUMMER TOMATO STACK

MAKES
4
SERVINGS

You can use just about any cheese with these tomato stacks, but I especially like locally produced goat, Cheddar, creamy brie, and blue of any kind.

8 thick slices ripe but firm tomatoes (approximately ½ inch thick)

Salt

Freshly ground black pepper

6 to 8 ounces cheese of your choice

2 to 3 teaspoons Dijon mustard

8 or more fresh basil leaves

½ cup unbleached all-purpose flour

3 large eggs, beaten

2 tablespoons extra-virgin olive oil, plus more for frying

2 cups fresh bread crumbs, toasted

2 tablespoons chopped fresh rosemary

Place the tomatoes on a baking sheet. Season with salt and pepper to taste.

Divide the cheese into fourths and place on top of 4 of the tomato slices—dollop or spread soft cheeses, slice and layer harder cheeses. Spread the mustard evenly on the other 4 tomato slices.

Place 1 or more basil leaves on top of each of the 8 tomato slices, pressing it gently onto the cheese or mustard.

Put the flour in a medium bowl. Combine the eggs and 2 tablespoons of the oil in another medium bowl. Combine the bread crumbs and rosemary in a pie plate and season generously with salt and pepper.

Dip the tomato stacks in the flour, then coat with the egg. Coat last with the bread crumbs.

Heat a thin layer of oil in a heavy skillet over medium heat. Add the tomatoes and cook for 3 minutes or until browned. Add more olive oil and turn the tomatoes to brown on the other side.

Serve warm or at room temperature.

THE LETTUCE WEDGE

My restaurant friends scoff at eating a wedge salad, but I have to admit that when I saw organically grown head lettuce for the first time, I let out a big old hurrah. Yes, I am from the East Coast, and now that one of my favorites—a wedge salad with all the fixings—can be made with pure ingredients, it shows up often when I cook at home. I make my own pickled beets, but they are easy to find in the canned food section and add so much to this version of the wedge.

⅓ cup extra-virgin olive oil

3 tablespoons rice vinegar

2 teaspoons stone-ground mustard

1 to 3 tablespoons chopped fresh herbs, such as tarragon, chives, oregano, or marjoram

1 garlic clove, minced

1 tablespoon sugar or honey (optional)

Salt

Freshly ground black pepper

1 medium head iceberg lettuce

8 slices bacon, cooked

6 ounces blue cheese, crumbled

4 hard-cooked large eggs, peeled and cut in half lengthwise

8 wedges pickled beets

In a small bowl, whisk together the oil, vinegar, mustard, herbs, garlic, and sugar, if using. Season generously with salt and pepper. Set aside at room temperature until ready to use.

Cut the iceberg into fourths. Place 1 wedge on each of 4 salad plates. Sprinkle with salt and pepper. Around each wedge, arrange 2 slices of bacon, one-fourth of the blue cheese, hard-cooked egg halves, and 2 wedges of pickled beets, and drizzle the whole thing with vinaigrette.

VARIATION
You can substitute ripe tomatoes for the beets.

MEXICAN CHOCOLATE FONDUE

I like to serve this dish with gingersnaps, figs, and organic strawberries for a lovely and scrumptious presentation. Surround it with fruit, cake cubes, and cookies for dipping.

2 cups whole milk

5 ounces unsweetened chocolate, grated

¾ cup sugar

1 cinnamon stick, broken in half

1 teaspoon vanilla extract

3 tablespoons brandy

In a small saucepan over medium heat, warm the milk, chocolate, sugar, and cinnamon stick. Cook, stirring often, for 5 minutes, or until the chocolate melts. Set aside for 15 minutes.

Return the saucepan to medium heat and bring the mixture to a simmer, whisking occasionally. Remove from the heat and discard the cinnamon stick. Add the vanilla and brandy. Serve in a fondue pot or individual heatproof ramekins set on a stand above a candle.

WATERMELON-ROSEMARY GRANITA

MAKES
8
SERVINGS

Watermelon is the epitome of summer, and I love it made into this cool, refreshing dessert for a hot summer day. The rosemary and lemon perk up the watermelon in a most pleasing way.

6 cups watermelon cubes, seeded

1 cup sugar

1 tablespoon fresh lemon juice

1 tablespoon finely chopped fresh rosemary

Put a 9-inch square metal baking pan in the freezer.

In a food processor or blender, purée enough of the watermelon to equal 3 cups.

In a small saucepan over medium-high heat, bring the sugar and 1 cup water to a boil. Continue boiling for 5 minutes, or until it thickens to a heavy syrup. Pour into a large bowl and cool completely.

When the syrup has cooled, add the watermelon purée, lemon juice, and rosemary. Pour into the frozen baking pan, cover with foil, and return it to the freezer. Freeze, stirring occasionally, for 3 hours, or until partially frozen.

Transfer the mixture to a food processor and process until smooth but still frozen. Return the mixture to the baking pan, cover, and freeze for 3 more hours, or until frozen.

Remove from the freezer 15 minutes before serving. Scoop into dessert bowls.

KITCHEN TIP

Granitas are smoothest when prepared in an ice-cream maker. If you have one, pour the mixture into the container of your ice-cream maker and prepare according to manufacturer's directions.

CREAM CHEESE–GLAZED SPONGE CAKE

This lovely light cake makes the perfect summer dessert. Use your favorite fruit juice to vary the recipe's main flavor while still producing a deliciously delicate cake. If you can't get organic fresh fruit juice, opt for frozen, which works just as well.

Cake

1 cup fruit juice, such as peach-mango, strawberry, guava, or orange

6 large eggs, separated

¾ teaspoon cream of tartar

1½ cups sugar

1½ cups sifted whole grain pastry flour

1 teaspoon baking powder

1 teaspoon ground cinnamon

½ teaspoon salt

4 tablespoons grated citrus zest, such as orange, lemon, or lime

Glaze

½ cup sugar

3 tablespoons boiling water

8 ounces cream cheese, softened

1 teaspoon vanilla extract

½ cup finely chopped walnuts

1 tablespoon grated citrus zest, such as orange, lemon, or lime

To make the cake: Preheat the oven to 350°F.

In a small saucepan over medium-high heat, cook the fruit juice for 10 minutes, or until reduced to ½ cup. Cool to room temperature.

Put the egg whites and cream of tartar in a large bowl. With an electric mixer on high speed, beat until soft peaks form. Gradually add ½ cup of the sugar, beating until stiff peaks form.

Put the egg yolks in another large bowl. Using the same beaters, beat the egg yolks on low speed until light and foamy. Gradually add the remaining 1 cup sugar and beat until creamy. Beat in the flour, baking powder, cinnamon, salt, fruit juice, and 4 tablespoons citrus zest just until blended. Pour the yolk mixture over the egg whites and gently fold in until well combined.

Pour the batter into an ungreased 10-inch tube pan. Bake for 45 minutes, or until a wooden pick inserted in the center comes out clean. Invert onto a heavy, long-necked bottle, such as a wine bottle, to cool completely.

To make the glaze: Meanwhile, put the sugar in a large bowl. Add the water and stir for 2 minutes, or until the sugar melts. Cool slightly. Add the cream cheese and vanilla extract. Beat with an electric mixer on medium speed until smooth and well blended.

When the cake is cool, invert onto a plate. Spread the glaze over the top of the cake. Sprinkle with walnuts and 1 tablespoon citrus zest.

NEWMAN'S OWN ORGANICS

We cater events for thousands and often serve Newman's Own Organics' wonderful snack foods for nibbling. The reactions of the guests are overwhelmingly positive, and our staff enjoys some healthy, behind-the-scenes munching, too.

Nell Newman, the company's cofounder, is a buddy of mine, and a remarkable grassroots leader in the organic food industry. The company continues to grow and offer more and more products. Because I know and trust Nell and her father, Paul Newman, we support Newman's Own Organics in any way we can. Oh, did I mention that Nell and I both love to fly-fish? But she is a champion, and I am a humble novice at the sport.

Nell and her business partner, Peter Meehan, started Newman's Own Organics: The Second Generation in 1993, as a division of Newman's Own. They were sure there was a market for organic snack foods, but they couldn't have anticipated just how fast the demand for their products would grow. The company started with pretzels and other snack foods and has expanded to include many other organic items: coffee, olive oil, balsamic vinegar, organic dried fruit, and pet food. Newman's Own Organics is now a separate company, but it is still closely tied to Newman's Own.

"'Great-tasting products that happen to be organic' is our slogan," Nell says. "It really says a lot about us." What Nell and other companies, both small and large, are realizing is that people want to know there is an identifiable person who cares about and monitors the food we purchase. Nell and her company are concerned about how the ingredients and products they offer are grown and how they taste.

When it comes to choosing which products to develop, Nell's and her partner Peter's personal preferences come into play. They produce the food they loved as kids, using high-quality organic ingredients.

Newman's Own Organics' products are certified by Oregon Tilth, one of the most respected certifying agencies in the country. The ingredients are grown on farms that have not used artificial fertilizers or pesticides for three years or more. The farms and processors have been certified by an independent third party. The products are sold nationwide in a number of mainstream supermarkets and many natural and health foods stores. The pet foods are sold in specialty pet stores and natural product stores.

Nell credits her parents for her desire to make a difference. "They taught me through their actions and the choices they've made," she states. "Paul Newman has been a role model in showing how an individual company can make a difference," Peter says. "Nell and I want to grow our business in the same way by producing good-tasting organic products with the goal of being able to make major contributions to a variety of charitable organizations and causes."

Paul Newman gives away all his royalty payments from Newman's Own Organics, after taxes, to educational and charitable organizations. Since 1982 he has given over $250 million to thousands of charities worldwide.

INDIAN SUMMER

At summer's end, when the memory of vacation fades, the routines of school and work urge me back to my kitchen. The days of casual summer dining are numbered, and leisurely meals at the table, surrounded by family and friends, seem important again. | Indian summer is a time of large platters overloaded with the bounty of just-picked goodness. It is a time to celebrate the harvest with family and friends and speak of fond memories of summer, as well as a time to honor and cherish the last summer crops, such as tomatoes and raspberries. I also give open-arm welcomes to baby acorn squash, broccoli, kale, chard, and other early fall arrivals. All earn prominent places on my dining room table. | Aware of the juxtaposition of seasons that Indian summer represents, I make conserving for the cold months ahead a priority, both at home and at my restaurant. My two food dryers are working nearly every night, the racks filled with tomatoes, peppers, eggplant, figs, and even berries. At the same time, herbs hang in bunches above my kitchen cabinets. Green tomatoes, cucumbers, beans, baby onions, and even Brussels sprouts are saved in jars filled with herbal or chile-infused vinegar. As the sweetness of summer disappears, I feel satisfied, knowing that I have created a kitchen that is ready for winter.

ROSEMARY-GRILLED FIGS

Some flavor combinations just seem to work on the palate, and figs and rosemary is one of them. That's why I like to cook figs on rosemary skewers, which lightly scent them during cooking.

4 rosemary skewers about 6 inches
    long (see Kitchen Tip) or 4 short
    wooden skewers

½ cup hearty red wine, such as
    Zinfandel or Cabernet

1 cup raspberries

1 teaspoon chopped fresh rosemary

1 tablespoon brown sugar

2 tablespoons balsamic vinegar

8 brown or green fresh figs

4 very thin slices lean prosciutto,
    halved lengthwise

Put the skewers in a shallow baking dish. Add the wine and soak for 30 minutes. Remove the skewers and set aside. Add the raspberries, rosemary, brown sugar, and vinegar to the wine and mash the berries with a fork. Set aside.

Prepare a medium charcoal fire or preheat a gas grill or a broiler to medium heat. Lightly oil a grill rack or broiler pan.

Meanwhile, wrap each fig with a half slice of the prosciutto. Thread 2 figs onto each skewer.

Place the figs on the rack or pan. Grill or broil the figs, turning often, for 5 minutes, or until they are warmed thoroughly. Serve with the raspberry sauce.

KITCHEN TIP

To make the rosemary skewers, choose 4 straight branches and trim them so they are about 6 inches long. Run your hand down each branch against the grain of the needles and remove them. Chop a few needles for the recipe (you'll need 1 teaspoon chopped). Put the rest in a jar to dry and use throughout the autumn season.

WARM BRIE WITH KUMQUATS

Kumquats appear often at the produce stands, but they are rarely used for anything but marmalade. This simple and seductive recipe was created spontaneously when I was a guest chef at an organic food show in Southern California. Not only is it easy, it is one of those dishes that has people begging for the recipe. I love ripened goat brie that is so soft, it oozes out of the rind. I splurge when bumping into a cheese maker at the farmers' market, spending whatever on a small piece of cheese that is gloriously delicious.

8 ounces Brie or Camembert cheese (1 or 2 rounds, depending on their weight)

8 ounces kumquats

1 tablespoon unsalted butter

1 small onion, thinly sliced

¼ cup packed brown sugar

¼ cup fruity white wine, such as Gewürztraminer, or white grape juice

⅛ teaspoon red-pepper flakes

Salt

1 loaf whole wheat Italian bread, thinly sliced (about 24 slices)

Put the cheese on a large plate and let come to room temperature.

Meanwhile, wash the kumquats, remove the stems, and slice them into rounds ⅛ inch thick. Put in a large bowl.

In a medium skillet over low heat, melt the butter. Add the onion and cook for 5 minutes, or until soft. Add the kumquats, cover, and simmer for 10 minutes, or until the kumquats are completely soft. Add the brown sugar, wine or grape juice, and red-pepper flakes and simmer for 15 minutes, or until the sauce is slightly thickened. Season with salt to taste. Cool slightly, then pour the sauce over the cheese. Serve immediately with the bread.

VARIATION

The kumquat sauce is delicious over sweets such as ice cream or angel food cake. Simply omit the onion and red-pepper flakes and increase the brown sugar to ½ cup.

STUFFED SHIITAKE MUSHROOMS

Though not a wild variety, shiitake mushrooms are grown organically and impart an earthy, musty flavor to any dish that calls for mushrooms. These stuffed mushrooms are great as an appetizer, or they can be served as a main course atop a bed of linguine tossed with olive oil and herbs.

3 tablespoons extra-virgin olive oil

2 tablespoons balsamic vinegar

2 garlic cloves, minced

2 tablespoons chopped fresh basil

½ teaspoon salt

¼ teaspoon freshly ground black pepper

1 pound large-capped shiitake or portabello mushrooms

1 small onion, finely chopped

1 small red bell pepper, finely chopped

2 tablespoons pine nuts, toasted

¼ cup red wine

¾ cup dry bread crumbs or finely crumbled fresh bread crumbs

1½ cups shredded Monterey Jack cheese (about 6 ounces)

Lightly oil the grill rack or oil a rack that fits in a baking dish. Prepare a medium charcoal fire or preheat a gas grill to medium heat, or preheat the oven to 400°F.

In a large bowl, combine the oil, vinegar, garlic, basil, salt, and black pepper. Spoon 2 tablespoons of the marinade into a medium skillet; set both aside.

Remove the stems from the mushroom caps. Chop the stems into small pieces. Put in a small bowl and add the onion, bell pepper, and toasted pine nuts.

Using a teaspoon, scrape out and discard the gills of the mushroom caps. Put the mushroom caps in the bowl of marinade, tossing them to coat all over.

Warm the marinade in the skillet over medium heat. Add the onion mixture and cook for 3 minutes, or until soft. Add the wine and continue cooking for 3 to 4 minutes. Remove the skillet from the heat, add the bread crumbs, and mix thoroughly.

Place the mushroom caps, stem side down, on the grill or on the rack in the baking dish. Grill or bake for 3 minutes. Remove the caps from the heat, place on a platter, and fill generously with the stuffing. Sprinkle an equal amount of cheese on top of each one. Return the mushrooms to the grill or oven, stuffed side up. Cover and grill for 5 to 8 minutes, or bake in the oven until warm and the cheese is browned.

LAST-OF-THE-SUMMER FETTUCCINE

It is always interesting to see what the staff of a restaurant chooses frequently for their evening meal. This is definitely an all-time favorite at Flea St. Café.

1 pound fresh fettuccine or similar pasta

¼ cup extra-virgin olive oil

1 small red onion, thinly sliced

½ red bell pepper, thinly sliced

2 large garlic cloves, minced

1 jalapeño chile pepper, seeded and minced

¼ cup tequila (optional)

2 large tomatoes, seeded and chopped

½ cup chopped fresh cilantro

2 tablespoons chopped fresh oregano

4 ounces feta cheese, crumbled

1 avocado, halved, pitted, peeled, and chopped

Salt

Freshly ground black pepper

Cook the fettuccine according to the package directions. Drain and transfer to a large bowl.

Meanwhile, heat the oil in a large skillet over medium-high heat. Add the onion and bell pepper and cook for 2 minutes. Add the garlic, chile pepper, and tequila, if using, and cook for 1 minute.

Add the tomatoes, cilantro, and oregano and cook for 3 minutes, or until the tomatoes are soft.

Stir the cheese and avocado into the sauce. Stir and season with salt and black pepper to taste. Add the sauce to the pasta and toss well.

SHELLING BEANS WITH TUNA

MAKES
4
SERVINGS

In early summer, shelling beans are best eaten fresh. When the pods are small and tender, they can be cooked whole, just like string beans. As they mature, the inner fresh beans are a delicious experience and take far less time to prepare than when they are dried. In my garden, I grow heirloom seeds from Seeds of Change, and beans are a favorite crop. We enjoy them from blossoms to tender bean pods to the dried beans we eat in winter.

8 ounces sushi-grade loin of tuna

Juice and grated zest of 1 lemon

2 garlic cloves, finely minced

Salt

Freshly ground black pepper

2 tablespoons olive oil

2 slices bacon, cut into small pieces

3 shallots, thinly sliced

1 pound tiny, tender whole shelling beans; or 1½ pounds medium shelling beans, shelled

1 tablespoon chopped fresh thyme

2 tablespoons thinly sliced fresh basil

In a small bowl, toss the tuna in the lemon juice with half the garlic. Season generously with salt and pepper.

Warm the oil in a medium skillet. Add the tuna and cook, turning once, until browned and to the desired doneness, but try to keep it as rare as possible, about 2 minutes per side. Remove the tuna to a platter.

To the same skillet, add the bacon, shallots, and the remaining half of the garlic, and cook for about 5 minutes, or until soft. Add the beans, lemon zest, thyme, and salt and pepper to taste. Cover and cook for 3 minutes, or until the beans are warm and tender.

While the beans are cooking, cut the tuna into ¼-inch slices. Spoon the beans onto one large platter or individual plates. Top with the sliced tuna. Sprinkle with fresh basil.

KITCHEN TIP

Tuna is delicious when cooked rare, and many restaurants serve it this way. If you're cooking it rare, be sure to purchase the highest quality tuna available, which is sushi-grade tuna, also known as Grade A.

ASIAN CHICKEN SALAD

4

SERVINGS

Chicken salads are extremely popular these days. When you infuse them with bold flavors such as ginger and Chinese mustard, the need for oil is greatly diminished, and the results are delicious.

½ cup seasoned rice vinegar

3 tablespoons soy sauce

1 teaspoon toasted sesame oil

1 to 2 tablespoons prepared hot
    Chinese mustard

2 tablespoons minced fresh ginger

2 green onions, thinly sliced

3 boneless, skinless chicken breast
    halves, cut into ¼-inch strips

2 cups bean sprouts

1 red bell pepper, thinly sliced

6 cups shredded Savoy cabbage (about
    1 smallish head)

1 tablespoon toasted sesame seeds

Preheat the oven to 400°F. Lightly oil a baking sheet.

In a large measuring cup, whisk together the vinegar, soy sauce, oil, mustard, ginger, and green onions. Pour half the dressing into a medium bowl.

Add the chicken to the bowl. Toss to coat and marinate for 10 minutes.

Meanwhile, in a large bowl, combine the sprouts, pepper, and cabbage. Toss with the remaining dressing. Allow to sit at room temperature for 20 minutes, tossing occasionally.

Place the chicken on the prepared baking sheet and bake for 10 minutes, or until cooked through and no longer pink. Cool slightly.

Add the chicken to the bowl with the cabbage mixture. Sprinkle with the sesame seeds and serve.

HARVEST POT ROAST

I love a good pot roast like this one. Be sure to save some to make sandwiches the next day. Slice the meat, smoosh some of the vegetables, and place between two slices of bread with sour cream or a smear of mustard.

1 large onion, cut into thick slices

2 carrots, cut into 1-inch pieces

12 ounces mushrooms, quartered

4 garlic cloves, minced

1 can (14½ ounces) diced tomatoes, drained

1 cup ketchup

2 tablespoons Dijon mustard

2 tablespoons Worcestershire sauce

1 chuck roast (2½ to 3 pounds), trimmed of all visible fat

¼ teaspoon salt

¼ teaspoon freshly ground black pepper

Combine the onion, carrots, mushrooms, garlic, and tomatoes in a slow cooker. In a small bowl, combine the ketchup, mustard, and Worcestershire sauce. Top the vegetables with half of the ketchup mixture.

Place the roast over the vegetables and sprinkle with the salt and pepper. Spread the remaining ketchup mixture over the roast. Cover and cook on low for 8 to 9 hours, or until the meat is very tender.

Let the meat rest for 10 minutes before slicing.

BONELESS LEG OF LAMB WITH HORSERADISH-MINT YOGURT AND DRIED CRANBERRIES

MAKES 8 TO 12 SERVINGS

Boneless leg of lamb is deliciously tender and juicy when cooked just until medium-rare. It is always tasty with horseradish cream, but here the cranberries and port add an extraordinarily rich flavor.

Juice of 1 lemon

3 tablespoons olive oil

5 garlic cloves, minced

3 tablespoons chopped fresh rosemary

2 teaspoons salt

1 teaspoon freshly ground black pepper

1 boneless butterflied leg of lamb (about 5 to 6 pounds)

$2/3$ cup whole milk yogurt

2 tablespoons grated red onion

3 tablespoons finely grated fresh horseradish, or 1 tablespoon prepared horseradish

3 tablespoons finely chopped fresh mint

1 cup ruby port

$2/3$ cup dried cranberries

$1/2$ teaspoon ground cinnamon

2 tablespoons brown sugar

Preheat the oven to 450°F.

In a small bowl, combine the lemon juice, olive oil, garlic, rosemary, salt, and pepper.

Open the lamb like a book, fat side down, on a work surface and rub most of the rosemary mixture evenly over the lamb. Fold the lamb back into its original shape and tie with string at 1-inch intervals. Pat the lamb dry and place in a roasting pan. Rub the remaining rosemary mixture over the lamb.

Roast for 20 minutes. Reduce the temperature to 350°F. Continue roasting the lamb until a thermometer inserted in the center registers 145°F (about 2 hours total cooking time for medium-rare). Remove from the oven and let rest for 15 minutes before slicing.

While the lamb is roasting, in a small bowl, combine the yogurt, red onion, horseradish, and mint. Season with salt and refrigerate until ready to use.

In a small sauce pan, over medium heat, bring the port to a simmer and add the cranberries, cinnamon, and sugar. Simmer for about 5 minutes to plump up the cranberries. With a slotted spoon, remove the cranberries to a small bowl. Continue to cook the sauce for 30 minutes, or until thick and syrupy and reduced by half. Pour over the cranberries.

To serve, slice the lamb and arrange on a platter or individual plates. Surround with the cranberries and sauce. Serve the horseradish cream alongside.

BUCKWHEAT NOODLES WITH WINTER SQUASH AND PORK LOIN

MAKES

6

SERVINGS

The toasty flavor of the buckwheat stands up beautifully to the rustic combination of the pork and squash. There are so many delicious, rich, and deep flavors in different squash varieties. Experiment and sample the many shapes, sizes, and colors available on the market at this time of the year.

2 tablespoons olive oil

¾ pound pork loin, cut into 1-inch cubes

1 medium butternut squash or sugar pumpkin, peeled, seeded, and cubed (about 2 cups)

2 large leeks (white part only), thinly sliced and thoroughly washed

2 garlic cloves, minced

½ cup raisins

1 cinnamon stick

1 cup chicken broth

1½ teaspoons paprika

1 tablespoon chopped fresh thyme, or 1 teaspoon dried

8 ounces dried buckwheat noodles (such as *soba*)

1½ cups sour cream

Heat the oil in a large skillet over medium heat. Add the pork and cook, turning frequently, for 6 minutes, or until cooked through. Remove to a large plate and keep warm.

Add the squash or pumpkin and leeks to the skillet and cook, stirring often, for 5 minutes, or until lightly browned. Add the garlic, raisins, cinnamon stick, broth, paprika, and thyme. Reduce the heat to low and simmer for 15 minutes, or until the squash is tender. Add the pork and simmer over low heat for 15 minutes.

Meanwhile, bring a large pot of water to a boil and cook the noodles according to the package directions. Drain and transfer to a large serving bowl.

Stir the sour cream into the pork mixture. Remove and discard the cinnamon stick. Pour the pork mixture over the noodles and serve.

SMOKED SAUSAGE, FUYU PERSIMMONS, WALNUTS, AND CITRUS DRESSING

MAKES
4
SERVINGS

Fuyu persimmons look like little flat pumpkins, while the Hachiyas are lantern-shaped. Fuyus are delicious raw, but I like to use them in any recipe that calls for apples. For a delicious, warming dish, I've tossed them with smoky sausage and a citrus vinaigrette.

1 pound Fuyu persimmons

½ cup fresh orange juice

¼ cup walnut or rice wine vinegar

¼ cup sugar

½ cup chopped red onion

2 tablespoons chopped fresh pineapple
    sage or thyme

2 tablespoons vegetable oil

1 pound smoked sausage, such as
    turkey or pork kielbasa

¾ cup walnuts, toasted

Do not peel the persimmons; just trim off the tops, and cut the fruit into ¼-inch wedges.

In a large bowl, whisk together the orange juice, vinegar, sugar, red onion, and pineapple sage or thyme. Add the persimmons and toss to coat. Set aside at room temperature, tossing occasionally.

In a large skillet over medium-high heat, warm the oil and cook the sausages until browned and cooked through. Remove from the heat and set aside. Add the persimmon mixture to the same skillet and cook for 4 minutes, or until heated through. Stir in the walnuts. Cut the sausages into large bite-size pieces.

Spoon the persimmons onto a serving platter or 4 plates and top with sausage.

OLD-FASHIONED CREAMED SPINACH

I was brought up in a small town east of Pittsburgh, where the shopping options for stylish clothes were limited. To solve the problem, my mom took me to the big city, where we often had lunch at one of the original Stouffer's restaurants. It was at that landmark that I first got hooked on this side dish of creamed spinach.

1 pound fresh spinach, or 2 packages (10 ounces each) frozen

4 thick slices bacon, chopped

2 tablespoons unsalted butter

½ red onion, finely chopped

2 tablespoons unbleached all-purpose flour

1½ cups milk

1 teaspoon Dijon mustard

¼ teaspoon salt

¼ teaspoon freshly grated nutmeg

2 hard-cooked large eggs, peeled and coarsely chopped

If using fresh spinach, in a covered saucepan, bring 1 inch of water to a boil. Put the spinach, in a steamer basket, into the saucepan. Cook the spinach until thoroughly wilted. Allow to cool. Using your hands, squeeze all excess juice out of the spinach. If using frozen spinach, thaw in a colander and squeeze out the excess water. Put the spinach on a cutting board and coarsely chop. Set aside in a bowl.

In a medium saucepan over medium-low heat, cook the bacon until crispy. Drain on paper towels. Pour off the bacon fat and wipe out the pan. Return the pan to the heat and melt the butter. Add the onion and cook over medium-low heat until softened. Stir in the flour and cook for 2 minutes, or until the mixture bubbles. Gradually whisk in the milk. Simmer, stirring frequently, over medium-low heat for 4 to 5 minutes, or until thickened. Stir in the mustard, salt, and nutmeg and remove from the heat. Allow to sit for 5 minutes.

To serve, pour the creamy sauce over the spinach and top with the bacon and eggs.

VARIATION

For a lovely brunch, serve the creamed spinach over toasted English muffins topped with poached eggs instead of hard-cooked eggs.

MASHED POTATO–STUFFED PEPPERS

This dish was created for a class I taught at Draeger's Culinary Center in Menlo Park, California. It literally made people smack their lips. I believe it was the creamy, luscious flavor of the combination of mashed potatoes and roasted peppers.

4 medium poblano or Anaheim chile peppers

2 garlic cloves, minced

2 tablespoons red wine vinegar

1 tablespoon extra-virgin olive oil

½ teaspoon salt

¼ teaspoon freshly ground black pepper

1 pound Yukon gold or any yellow-fleshed potatoes, peeled and cut into large chunks

2 tablespoons chopped fresh chives

4 ounces cream cheese

¼ to ½ cup milk

½ cup shredded Cheddar or Monterey Jack cheese (about 2 ounces)

Preheat the oven to 375°F.

Cut the chile peppers in half lengthwise, remove the seeds and stems, and scrape away most of the white membranes.

In a medium bowl, combine the garlic, vinegar, oil, salt, and black pepper. Toss the chile peppers in the bowl to thoroughly coat. Place, cut side down, on a baking sheet and bake for 20 to 30 minutes, or until the peppers are tender.

Meanwhile, bring a large pot of salted water to a boil and cook the potatoes for 15 minutes, or

until tender. Drain and transfer to a large bowl. Mash the potatoes with the chives. Cut the cream cheese into pieces and add to the potatoes, allowing it to melt. Mash it in with the potatoes. Continue mashing and add enough milk to make the potatoes smooth and creamy.

Turn the peppers cut side up on the baking sheet. Mound the mashed potatoes in the baked peppers. Top with the shredded cheese. Bake for 15 minutes, or until lightly browned.

WHOLE GRAIN SALAD WITH CUCUMBER AND FETA

MAKES **4** SERVINGS

There are so many wonderful organic whole grains on the market, and this combination of flavors would work well with most of them. At our catering company, this salad, made with milo or wheat berries, is one of the most popular. Note that the recipe calls for cooked grains because the cooking times and ratios of grain to water vary so much from one grain to the next. Consult the directions on the package or search for information on the Internet, as many of us now do.

2 cups cooked hearty whole grains, such as milo, wheat berries, bulgur, spelt, or barley

2 green onions, chopped

1 medium cucumber, peeled, seeded, and finely chopped

2 tablespoons chopped fresh dill

1 garlic clove, minced

½ jalapeño or another hot chile pepper, minced

2 tablespoons extra-virgin olive oil

Juice of ½ lemon, or more to taste

3 ounces feta cheese, crumbled

Salt

Freshly ground black pepper

In a medium bowl, toss together the grains, green onions, cucumber, dill, garlic, jalapeño, oil, and lemon juice, and season with salt and pepper. Allow to sit at room temperature for 15 minutes. Stir in the feta cheese. Serve at room temperature or chilled.

KITCHEN TIP

Milo is grain sorghum, a gluten-free grain native to Africa and Asia. This small round berry varies in color from light brown to white. It has a slightly nutty flavor and can be eaten like popcorn, cooked into porridge, ground into flour for baked goods, or brewed into beer.

FRISÉE WITH SPICY MAPLE PECANS

This interesting salad is wonderful as a first course, side dish, or served as a bed beneath grilled chicken or roasted game hen.

1 cup pecan halves

¼ cup pure maple syrup

½ teaspoon freshly ground black pepper

½ teaspoon ground red pepper (cayenne)

½ teaspoon salt

1 garlic clove

¼ red onion, chopped

2 tablespoons extra-virgin olive oil

2 ounces feta cheese, crumbled

2 to 3 tablespoons red wine vinegar

1½ teaspoons sugar

1 teaspoon Dijon mustard

2 medium heads frisée, cut into bite-size pieces

Preheat the oven to 400°F. Lightly oil a baking sheet.

In a small bowl, combine the pecans with the maple syrup. Sprinkle with the black pepper, red pepper, and salt. Toss to coat well. Spread out in a single layer on the prepared baking sheet. Bake the nuts, tossing frequently, for 5 minutes, or until lightly toasted. Transfer the nuts to a rack to cool.

In a food processor or blender, combine the garlic and onion. With the motor running, gradually add the oil and purée just until blended. Add the cheese, vinegar, sugar, and mustard and purée until well blended. Transfer to a serving bowl.

Mound the frisée onto 6 plates. Top with the nuts. Serve the dressing on the side.

GREEN TOMATOES AND PEPPERS

When the days of autumn diminish the heat of summer, and the last few tomatoes on my vines have no chance of ripening, I toss them, green and unripened, into a salad with red bell peppers, which linger on the vine, too, and (unlike the tomatoes) keep getting sweeter. The dish is great on its own or served alongside seafood or chicken. This lively combination would also be delicious tossed with a little extra olive oil and whole wheat pasta.

¼ cup olive oil or vegetable oil, such as avocado

2 tablespoons red wine vinegar

1 to 2 garlic cloves, minced

¼ cup chopped fresh cilantro

1 teaspoon ground cumin

½ teaspoon chili powder

1 small red onion, thinly sliced

2 medium green tomatoes, seeded and cut into ½-inch pieces

1 medium red bell pepper, seeded and cut into ¼-inch pieces

Salt

Freshly ground black pepper

Sugar (optional)

In a medium bowl, combine the oil, vinegar, garlic, cilantro, cumin, chili powder, and onion. Allow to sit at room temperature for at least 30 minutes.

Add the tomatoes and pepper, tossing to coat well. Season with salt and pepper to taste and add sugar if desired.

APPLESAUCE OATMEAL COOKIES

The applesauce in this recipe keeps the cookies moist, just as it does in applesauce cake.

1 cup whole grain pastry flour

1 teaspoon baking powder

¾ teaspoon salt

½ teaspoon ground cinnamon

½ cup (1 stick) unsalted butter, softened

1 cup packed brown sugar

1 large egg

½ cup applesauce

¾ teaspoon vanilla extract

2 cups rolled oats

½ cup raisins (optional)

¼ cup coarsely chopped walnuts or pecans (optional)

Preheat the oven to 375°F. Line a baking sheet with parchment paper.

In medium bowl, combine the flour, baking powder, salt, and cinnamon. Set aside.

In a large bowl with an electric mixer on medium speed, beat the butter and brown sugar until light and fluffy. Add the egg, applesauce, and vanilla extract. Gradually beat in the flour mixture. With a wooden spoon, stir in the oats, raisins, and nuts, if using.

Drop the dough by heaping teaspoonfuls onto the prepared baking sheet. Bake for 10 minutes, or until lightly browned.

UPSIDE-DOWN PEAR CHOCOLATE CAKE

This cake was an experiment that turned into one of the most popular desserts at the Flea St. Café. I am not a chocoholic, but I eat this confection with abandon.

1¾ cups whole grain pastry flour

1¾ cups sugar

¾ cup unsweetened cocoa powder

2 teaspoons baking soda

1 teaspoon baking powder

¾ teaspoon salt

2 large eggs

¾ cup strong brewed coffee, cooled

¾ cup buttermilk (see Organic Tip on page 38)

½ cup vegetable oil

1 teaspoon vanilla extract

2 to 3 large pears, peeled, cored, and sliced

Preheat the oven to 375°F. Lightly oil a 10-inch cake pan. Line the pan with parchment paper and lightly oil the paper.

In a medium bowl, combine the flour, sugar, cocoa, baking soda, baking powder, and salt.

In large bowl, whisk together the eggs, coffee, buttermilk, oil, and vanilla extract. Gradually stir the flour mixture into the egg mixture. Mix until thoroughly blended.

Line the bottom of the cake pan with the pears in a circular design. Pour the batter on top of the pears. Bake for 55 minutes, or until a wooden pick inserted in the center comes out clean.

Place on a rack and let sit for 10 minutes. Run a metal spatula around the sides of the cake to loosen them. Invert the pan onto a plate. Using the handle of a knife, vigorously tap the top of the pan, even shaking it a bit, to loosen the cake. Leave the pan over the cake for 15 minutes. Remove the pan and let the cake cool completely.

COCONUT CUSTARD TARTLETS WITH HERB CRUSTS

Adding a hint of herbs to the crust brings a lovely touch to these little tarts. When I make these, I prepare the custard and crusts separately and assemble the tarts just before serving.

Crusts

2½ cups whole grain pastry flour, plus extra for sprinkling work surface

¼ teaspoon freshly grated nutmeg

3 tablespoons chopped fresh thyme

¾ teaspoon salt

1 cup (2 sticks) cold unsalted butter

6 to 10 tablespoons milk

Custard

3 large egg yolks

¾ cup sugar

Pinch of salt

3 tablespoons cornstarch

2½ cups whole milk

½ whole vanilla bean

1½ cups unsweetened coconut flakes, toasted

3 tablespoons unsalted butter

To make the crusts: Preheat the oven to 425°F.

In a medium bowl, combine the flour, nutmeg, thyme, and salt. Grate the butter into the mixture. Using your hands or a pastry blender, work the butter into the flour mixture. Gradually add enough of the milk so that the mixture can be shaped into a ball.

Divide the dough into 12 pieces and roll each into a small ball. On a well-floured board, flatten into disks and roll into 8-inch circles with a rolling pin, using additional flour to keep the dough from sticking to the board.

If you are using tart pans, press the dough into the pans with your fingers. Then, using your thumb and index finger, lightly pinch or roll in the dough overhanging the edges of each pan to form a pastry edge. Place the tart shells on a baking sheet.

If you are making free-form crusts, line the baking sheet with parchment paper. Arrange the circles of dough on the baking sheets and roll in and crimp the edges.

Bake the tartlets for 15 minutes, or until lightly browned. Remove to a rack to cool.

To make the custard: Meanwhile, in a medium bowl, whisk together the egg yolks, sugar, salt, and cornstarch. Combine the milk and vanilla bean in a medium saucepan. Bring to a simmer over medium heat and slowly whisk in the egg mixture. Stir in 1¼ cups of the coconut, reserving the rest for garnish.

Cook the mixture over medium heat, stirring constantly, for 10 minutes, or until thickened. Remove the saucepan from the heat. Remove and discard the vanilla bean. Whisk in the butter.

Transfer the coconut custard to a bowl. Cover with waxed paper and refrigerate for 2 hours, or until chilled.

To serve, fill the shells with the custard. Sprinkle with the remaining ¼ cup coconut.

ORGANIC VALLEY FAMILY OF FARMS AND ORGANIC PRAIRIE

When I was researching organic companies and compiling a list of eight to feature in this book, everyone I asked suggested Organic Valley. CEO George Siemon leads a nationwide organization of small family dairies, cooperatively owned and operated. No other organic company has been as successful at upholding sustainable ethics for the environment, for farmers, and consumers.

Organic Valley began in 1988 in Wisconsin with just seven farmers. They shared a love of the land and a belief that a sustainable approach to agriculture was needed for family farms and rural communities to survive. At a time when nearly 2,000 farms were going out of business every week, these seven farmers set out to create a way for the family farm to flourish.

Their solution has grown into the largest organic farming cooperative in North America. CROPP Cooperative (Cooperative Regions of Organic Producer Pools) and the Organic Valley brand have become one of the largest pioneering organic brands in the nation. From the seven founding Wisconsin farmers, the cooperative has expanded from California to Maine, and in one Canadian province. Today, the cooperative's farmers represent nearly 10 percent of the United State's certified Organic farming community.

Though it has grown, Organic Valley remains true to its roots. It is the only national organic brand to be solely owned and operated by organic farmers. Part of the cooperative's success is due to the fact that as farmer-owners, members pay themselves a stable, equitable, and sustainable price for their products. In an era of rising and falling agricultural prices, the family farmers who produce Organic Valley milk, juice, eggs, and produce can rely on a stable, living wage to stay in business in their home regions. The same is true for Organic Prairie farmers, who raise meat and are part of the CROPP cooperative. Farmers from all over the world trek regularly to CROPP's headquarters in rural La Farge, Wisconsin, to learn what makes its cooperative model work.

CROPP is a relationship-based business. It does everything from creating partnerships with its farmers and milk handlers to contracting with production plants and shipping companies. In addition, it helps to support nonprofit organizations. When it was time to build an employee headquarters, CROPP chose to remain in its home town of La Farge. It is currently building a distribution center in the Cashton Greens Business Park, a new "green" business park that will produce alternative forms of energy such as wind, biodiesel, and biomass conversion. Both buildings were designed to be environmentally sustainable, in keeping with the cooperative member's values of preserving the land on which they and their children live.

Being farmer-owned and independent has allowed CROPP Cooperative to stay true to its mission—keeping family farmers farming. Sharing the vision of truly sustainable agricultural practices, Organic Valley and Organic Prairie farmers go beyond organic standards with their stewardship of the earth. They are at the heart of the organic revolution.

AUTUMN HARVEST

I don't need a calendar to alert me when autumn arrives. I know it on my daily walks, when the mornings are cold and the fallen leaves crunch beneath my feet. Inside, my feet, bare a short time ago, are now covered with socks, and the closed windows get steamy as the cold outdoors collides with the warmth from my kitchen. | At the farmers' market, the selection of fresh produce has dwindled. Even in your own garden, you might be lucky if you find remnants of summer crops, perhaps a few tomatoes still clinging to a vine or a handful of raspberries. This is the time when fall crops hit their prime in color, taste, and texture. Squash, pumpkins, cabbage, tangerines, apples, pomegranates, and persimmons are treasured. | During autumn, I try to use every fresh ingredient available, orchestrating dishes that combine the fall harvest with preserved foods. As always, I do my best to use what grows as close as possible to my home or willingly pay extra for organic and pesticide-free produce grown elsewhere. | I enjoy creating robust dishes, indulging myself in rich, stick-to-the-ribs foods that protect me from the cold. I relish the challenge of cutting a rebellious winter squash or figuring out creative ways to use parsnips and celery root. | Autumn is the time to reach for dried, canned, and frozen ingredients from your pantry shelves and freezer. Satisfy your hunger for a tomato dish by using ones that you canned, dried, or froze a few months ago.

CELERY ROOT, POTATO, AND APPLE SOUP

This creamy soup has no real cream, but is rich with earthy flavors. It makes sense that we would want root vegetables to be grown organically. Since they are grown completely underground, it's essential that they grow in pure soil that has not been touched by pesticides or anything artificial or possibly harmful.

2 tablespoons olive oil

1 medium onion, finely chopped

½ cup dry white wine

5 cups chicken or vegetable broth, or more if you like a thinner soup

1 large russet potato, peeled and chopped

1 large celery root (celeriac), peeled and chopped (about 1 pound)

1½ tablespoons chopped fresh thyme

1 apple, grated

Salt

Freshly ground black pepper

1 cup shredded Cheddar cheese (about 4 ounces; optional)

½ cup pecans, toasted (optional)

In a large pot over medium-high heat, warm the oil and cook the onion for 4 minutes, or until soft. Add the wine and cook for 3 minutes longer. Add the broth, potato, celery root, and thyme. Bring to a boil over high heat. Reduce the heat to medium-low, cover, and simmer for 1 hour, or until the vegetables are very soft.

Working in batches if necessary, transfer the mixture to a food processor or blender. Process until smooth. Stir in the apple and pour back into the pot. Warm for 15 minutes to let the flavors marry, and season with salt and pepper to taste.

To serve, ladle into soup bowls and top each serving with the cheese and pecans, if using.

KITCHEN TIP

I like to make soups a day or two ahead so the flavors can meld perfectly. Try making some on the weekend and refrigerate until later in the week for a speedy supper. Don't forget a tossed salad and crusty bread.

BROCCOLI AND GINGER POT STICKERS

These versatile dumplings make a delicious appetizer. Consider substituting other autumn vegetables for the broccoli, such as cauliflower, cabbage, or kale.

Dipping Sauce

4 tablespoons soy sauce

3 tablespoons rice wine vinegar

2 tablespoons brown sugar

½ teaspoon toasted sesame oil

½ teaspoon red-pepper flakes

Pot Stickers

1 tablespoon olive oil

1 small red onion, coarsely grated

1½ cups finely chopped fresh or thawed frozen broccoli

1 cup vegetable or chicken broth

1 garlic clove, minced

1 tablespoon grated fresh ginger

24 round wonton wrappers

2 green onions, thinly sliced

1 teaspoon black sesame seeds (optional)

To make the dipping sauce: In a small bowl, combine 3 tablespoons of the soy sauce, the vinegar, brown sugar, sesame oil, and red-pepper flakes, and set aside.

To make the pot stickers: Heat the olive oil in a large skillet over medium heat. Add the red onion and cook for 1 minute, or until soft. Add the broccoli and broth. Cover and cook for 10 minutes, or until the broccoli is very soft and all the broth has evaporated. Add the garlic, ginger, and the remaining 1 tablespoon soy sauce and cook for 2 minutes. Drain off any excess liquid and cool.

Bring a large skillet of salted water to a boil over high heat. Reduce the heat to low, cover, and simmer.

Place 1 teaspoon of broccoli filling in the center of each wonton wrapper. Moisten the outer edges of each wrapper with water and tightly seal using a wonton press or your fingers.

Working in batches if necessary, place the wontons in the simmering water for 2 minutes, or until heated through. Drain and place on a platter with the dipping sauce. Sprinkle with the green onions and sesame seeds (if desired).

WILD, WILD PASTA

MAKES
8
SERVINGS

This great cool-weather pasta is a favorite in my restaurant Flea St. Café, reappearing each year as soon as the last of the fresh tomatoes disappear. It's a great way to use leftover wild rice, so make a double batch and set some aside for this quick dish.

1 pound fettuccine

¼ cup extra-virgin olive oil

2 garlic cloves, minced

1 to 2 jalapeño chile peppers, seeded and finely chopped

¼ cup dry white wine

8 ounces wild mushrooms, such as chanterelle, black trumpet, lobster, or porcini

1½ cups cooked wild rice

6 ounces feta cheese, crumbled

½ cup coarsely chopped oil-packed sun-dried tomatoes, drained

2 tablespoons finely chopped fresh marjoram, or 1 tablespoon dried

1 tablespoon grated lemon zest

Salt

Freshly ground black pepper

Chopped fresh Italian parsley

Cook the pasta according to package directions. Drain and transfer to a large bowl.

Meanwhile, heat the oil in a large skillet over medium heat. Add the garlic and chile pepper and cook for 1 minute. Add the wine and cook for 1 minute. Add the mushrooms and cook, stirring frequently, for 3 to 4 minutes, wilting the mushrooms slightly. Remove from the heat and stir in the rice, cheese, tomatoes, marjoram, and lemon zest. Season with salt and black pepper to taste.

Add the mushroom sauce to the pasta and toss to coat. Garnish with parsley.

SPAGHETTI SQUASH WITH **CLAM SAUCE**

MAKES
4
SERVINGS

Spaghetti squash has a wonderful texture. The cooked strands look like spaghetti and seem to hold up well under any sauce that you might use with pasta. The clam sauce is also good served over other winter squash, such as butternut or acorn.

1 spaghetti squash (about 1½ pounds)

2 tablespoons extra-virgin olive oil

2 tablespoons unsalted butter

2 large garlic cloves, minced

1 can (2 ounces) anchovies, drained and chopped

2 tablespoons capers

1 tablespoon grated lemon zest

36 clams, such as littleneck, Manila, or cherrystone, scrubbed

1 bottle (8 ounces) clam juice

½ cup dry vermouth

1 to 2 teaspoons red-pepper flakes (optional)

2 tablespoons chopped fresh Italian parsley

Salt

Freshly ground black pepper

¼ cup grated Asiago, Romano, or Parmesan cheese (about 1 ounce)

Preheat the oven to 375°F. Cut the squash in half lengthwise. Scrape out and discard the seeds. Place the squash, cut side down, in a heavy baking dish and add 1 cup water. Bake for 35 minutes, or until tender. Set aside just until cool enough to handle.

When cool, using a fork, scrape crosswise to pull the strands of squash away from the shell. Transfer to a large bowl.

While the squash is still baking, heat the oil and butter in a large skillet over medium heat. Add the garlic, anchovies, capers, and lemon zest. Cook, stirring frequently, for 5 minutes and set aside.

Once the spaghetti squash is cooked, add the clams, clam juice, and vermouth to the skillet with the garlic mixture. Place over high heat and bring to a boil. Reduce the heat to low, cover, and simmer for 5 minutes, or until the clams open. Discard any unopened clams. Add the red-pepper flakes, if using, and parsley and season with salt and pepper to taste. Pour the sauce over the spaghetti squash.

Sprinkle with the cheese.

PRAWN-STUFFED PETRALE SOLE

MAKES

6

SERVINGS

When buying petrale sole or any seafood that might have been caught by trolling, ask your fishmonger for information on how the fish was caught. Petrale sole is on the questionable-seafood list in the Monterey Bay Aquarium's Seafood Watch guide; at my restaurant, we make sure the fish we purchase is line-caught. Also, when you purchase fish, it may be labeled fresh, but could have been out of the water as long as two weeks. Sometimes the most sustainable choice is fish that has been harvested, cleaned, and flash-frozen on board the fishing boat.

8 ounces prawns (large shrimp),
    peeled and coarsely chopped
    (see Organic Tip)

3 ounces smoked salmon, coarsely chopped

2 green onions, finely chopped

3 tablespoons cold unsalted butter, grated

1 tablespoon grated fresh ginger

1 pound petrale sole fillet, or a similar
    flat, small, delicate fish

Salt

Freshly ground black pepper

2 tablespoons olive oil

Preheat the oven to 375°F. Lightly oil a baking sheet.

In a medium bowl, combine the prawns, salmon, onions, butter, and ginger.

Cut the sole into 6 pieces, each about 5 by 2 inches. Lay flat on a cutting board and season with salt and pepper to taste. Divide the prawn mixture evenly among the fillets, spreading it over each one.

Roll up like a jelly roll. Flatten each side and brush generously with olive oil. Place the fillets on the prepared baking sheet and bake for 20 minutes, or until the fish flakes when tested with a fork.

ORGANIC TIP
Because of the large market for shrimp, too often they are produced without respect for the environment. When buying shrimp, be sure to ask questions about where they come from, how they are cultivated if farm-raised, or how they are caught if wild, to ensure that you are purchasing sustainable shrimp.

CHICKEN WITH APRICOT-ALMOND STUFFING

I prefer to roast my stuffing separately from the bird. It lessens the possibility of overcooking the meat and produces a crisp, dense stuffing. Since the stuffing is my favorite part of this dish anyway, sometimes I don't even bother with the chicken!

Chicken

1 roasting chicken (3 to 4 pounds)

1 tablespoon olive oil

¼ teaspoon salt

¼ teaspoon freshly ground black pepper

3 teaspoons paprika

Stuffing

3 tablespoons unsalted butter

2 celery ribs, chopped

1 onion, chopped

4 ounces mushrooms, sliced

1 tablespoon ground sage

⅓ cup slivered almonds, chopped

4 to 6 dried apricots, coarsely chopped

1½ pounds hearty whole grain or semolina bread, torn into pieces

2 large eggs, beaten

2 to 3 cups chicken broth

½ teaspoon salt

¼ teaspoon freshly ground black pepper

Preheat the oven to 475°F. Lightly butter a 2-quart baking dish.

To make the chicken: Rub the chicken with the oil and season with the salt, pepper, and paprika. Place on a rack in a roasting pan and roast for 20 minutes. Reduce the heat to 375°F and continue roasting for 1 hour, or until a thermometer inserted in the breast registers 180°F and the juices run clear. Let sit for 10 minutes before carving.

To make the stuffing: Meanwhile, melt the butter in a medium skillet over medium-high heat. Add the celery, onion, and mushrooms and cook for 5 minutes, or until soft. Add the sage, almonds, and apricots and cook for 1 minute. Remove from the heat.

Put the bread in a large bowl and toss with the mushroom mixture. Add the eggs, stirring to blend well. Add 2 cups of the broth, the salt, and pepper, and stir well. Add another 1 cup broth if a moister stuffing is preferred. Transfer to the prepared baking dish.

Place in the oven during the last 30 minutes of the chicken's roasting time. Bake until the stuffing puffs up and the top is light brown.

VARIATION

This recipe is great for Thanksgiving. To roast a turkey, double the chicken seasonings and prepare as you would the chicken. Roast a 12- to 14-pound bird for 3 to 3½ hours, or until a thermometer inserted in a breast registers 180°F and the juices run clear. Let sit for 10 minutes before carving. Prepare the stuffing as directed, doubling it if necessary.

CHÈVRE-STUFFED CHICKEN THIGHS

We need to use all parts of the chicken, even though, in the West, we have become accustomed to eating only the breast. If you use boned chicken thighs, this recipe can be prepared and on the table within 30 minutes. These chicken thighs are delicious served over hearty grains, such as barley or brown rice.

4 ounces soft goat cheese, such as chèvre

¼ cup currants or raisins

2 tablespoons dry bread crumbs

1 tablespoon chopped fresh chives

1 tablespoon chopped fresh oregano, or 1 teaspoon dried

½ teaspoon freshly ground black pepper

1 tablespoon olive oil

1 tablespoon mixed dried Italian herbs

½ teaspoon salt

8 chicken thighs

Preheat the oven to 400°F.

In a small bowl, combine the cheese, currants or raisins, bread crumbs, chives, oregano, and pepper.

In another small bowl, combine the oil, Italian herbs, and salt.

Place the chicken on a rack in a roasting pan. Lift the skin of each thigh and place one-eighth of the cheese mixture under the skin. Brush the skin with the oil mixture.

Roast for 30 minutes, or until a thermometer inserted in the thickest portion registers 170°F and the juices run clear.

SHORT RIBS WITH BABY TURNIPS

MAKES
6
SERVINGS

Organic and grass-fed beef are finally more widely available. Short ribs are much sought after these days, but this recipe also works well with chuck or any pot roast. Once you begin cooking with meats that are not treated with artificial hormones or antibiotics, you will notice a difference in the depth of taste and texture. I find that organic meats have much more flavor than conventional ones.

3 pounds beef short ribs

2 tablespoons garam masala

Salt

Freshly ground black pepper

6 garlic cloves, chopped

8 shallots

2 carrots, finely chopped

2 celery ribs, finely chopped

1 cup hearty red wine, such as Zinfandel

3 to 4 cups vegetable or chicken broth

1 can (14½ ounces) diced tomatoes with their juice

4 sprigs fresh thyme

4 sprigs fresh Italian parsley

2 bay leaves

2 teaspoons ground coriander

1 teaspoon ground cloves

2 bunches baby turnips (about 24 turnips)

Preheat the oven to 450°F.

Season the ribs with the garam masala and a pinch of salt and pepper. Place in a large roasting pan and roast for 45 minutes, or until the meat is browned, turning it once.

Reduce the heat to 375°F. Add the garlic, shallots, carrots, celery, wine, 3 cups of the broth, tomatoes with juice, thyme, parsley, bay leaves, coriander, cloves, 1 teaspoon salt, and 1 teaspoon pepper. Roast, uncovered, for 1½ hours, or until the meat is tender but not yet falling off the bone.

Wash the turnips and, if they are larger than about 2 inches in diameter, cut them in half or into wedges. Add to the ribs. Spoon the sauce over the turnips and ribs. Add another 1 cup broth if the sauce is too thick. Roast for 1 hour, or until the turnips and meat are tender.

Using tongs or a slotted spoon, remove the ribs and turnips to a serving platter.

Remove and discard the bay leaves and thyme sprigs in the sauce. Working in batches if necessary, pour the sauce into a food processor or blender. Purée until smooth.

Pour the sauce over the ribs and turnips and serve.

PORK CHOPS WITH DRIED BERRY–PORT SAUCE

Reminiscent of the cherry glaze traditionally served with meat, this rich sauce is a delicious complement to flavorful pork chops. For a change of pace, try the sauce over smoked pork chops or even ham steak.

3 whole cloves, or ½ teaspoon ground cloves

3 whole black peppercorns

1 bay leaf

1 cinnamon stick

1½ cups dried berries, such as blackberries, raspberries, or blueberries

1 cup ruby port

3 tablespoons brown sugar

1 tablespoon Dijon mustard

2 tablespoons unsalted butter

4 rib pork chops

Combine the cloves, peppercorns, bay leaf, and cinnamon stick in a piece of cheesecloth or a small gauze bag. Tie with kitchen twine to seal. Put in a medium saucepan along with the berries, port, 1 cup water, brown sugar, and mustard. Bring to a boil over high heat. Reduce the heat to low and simmer for 1 hour, or until the liquid is reduced by half and thickened slightly. Remove and discard the spice bag.

Melt the butter in a large skillet over medium-high heat. Add the chops and cook for 8 minutes, turning once, or until a thermometer inserted in the center of a chop registers 160°F and the juices run clear.

Serve the pork chops with the sauce.

AUTUMN VEGETABLE GRATIN

The thinner you slice the vegetables, the better. I use a tool called a mandoline, which is a small tabletop slicer. You can find it in most cookware shops or catalogs. Otherwise, use a very sharp knife, take your time, and you will get the same results.

¼ cup unbleached all-purpose flour

¼ cup brown sugar

1 cup shredded Cheddar cheese (about 4 ounces)

1 teaspoon salt

½ teaspoon freshly ground black pepper

1½ pounds winter squash, such as butternut, buttercup, Hokkaido, or acorn, peeled and thinly sliced

1 onion, thinly sliced

2 golden flesh potatoes, such as Yukon gold, peeled and thinly sliced

1 fennel bulb, peeled and thinly sliced

2 to 3 cups milk, as needed

½ cup grated Parmesan cheese (about 2 ounces)

Preheat the oven to 350°F. Oil a 2-quart baking dish.

In a small bowl, combine the flour, brown sugar, Cheddar, salt, and pepper. Set aside.

Layer one-third of the squash, onion, potatoes, and fennel in the prepared baking dish. Dust with one-third of the flour mixture. Repeat the layers two more times, finishing with the flour mixture. Pour enough of the milk over all to cover the potatoes and come two-thirds of the way up the sides of the baking dish. Press down slightly to moisten all the ingredients, and sprinkle with the Parmesan.

Bake for 1½ hours, or until the vegetables are very tender and the gratin is golden brown. If the top browns too quickly, cover loosely with foil. Let stand for 15 minutes before serving.

KITCHEN TIP

For a lighter version of this luscious dish, use vegetable or chicken broth instead of milk. I like to make this the day before serving, as the flavors seem to improve.

ROASTED PARSNIPS

I often roast root vegetables, and next to beets and onions, parsnips are my favorite. Their creamy sweetness seems to be enhanced in the oven. I cover my baking sheet with parchment paper because the sugar in the parsnips can make cleaning a chore.

1 pound parsnips, peeled and cut into 3-inch sticks

2 medium leeks, cleaned and sliced into ½-inch rounds

2 tablespoons olive oil

2 garlic cloves, minced

1 teaspoon chopped fresh oregano

¼ teaspoon salt

¼ teaspoon freshly ground black pepper

Preheat the oven to 375°F. Line a baking sheet with parchment paper.

Put the parsnips and leeks in a large bowl. Sprinkle with the oil, garlic, oregano, salt, and pepper. Toss to coat well. Spread out on the prepared baking sheet.

Roast, turning occasionally, for 30 minutes, or until the parsnips are tender and lightly browned.

BARLEY–SWEET POTATO HASH

I make this hash and top it with a couple of fresh eggs, poached or fried over easy. The yolks seep into the hash, and the only thing left to reach for is the bottle of hot sauce.

½ cup pearl barley

2 tablespoons vegetable or light olive oil

1 small onion, coarsely chopped

1 sweet potato, peeled and cut into ¼-inch pieces

2 cups vegetable broth

Salt

Freshly ground black pepper

Put the barley in a medium saucepan over medium heat. Cook, shaking the pan often, for 5 minutes, or until toasted. Remove the barley to a bowl.

In the same saucepan, heat the oil over medium heat. Add the onion and sweet potato and cook, stirring occasionally, for 5 minutes, or until lightly browned. Add the barley and broth. Bring to a boil over high heat. Reduce the heat to medium-low, cover, and simmer, stirring occasionally, for 30 minutes, or until the barley is tender but still firm and the liquid is absorbed. Season generously with salt and pepper.

VARIATIONS

I like to stir ham, smoked tofu, or cooked chicken or shrimp into a bowl of this hash to make a hearty meal.

BITTER GREENS
WITH DEVILED EGGS

Bitter greens piled next to irresistible deviled eggs is an innovative way to combine hard-cooked eggs with a salad.

Vinaigrette

¼ cup extra-virgin olive oil

3 tablespoons red wine vinegar

½ teaspoon Dijon mustard, or more to taste

2 tablespoons chopped fresh oregano

½ cup chopped green onions

Salt

Freshly ground pepper

Deviled Eggs

7 hard-cooked large eggs

1 teaspoon sugar

½ teaspoon Dijon mustard

3½ tablespoons mayonnaise

1½ tablespoons sweet pickle relish

1 tablespoon finely grated red onion

Salt

Freshly ground pepper

1 pound bitter greens, such as frisée, radicchio, or escarole

Paprika for garnish

To make the vinaigrette: In a small bowl, combine the olive oil, vinegar, mustard, oregano, and green onions. Season generously with salt and pepper. Set aside at room temperature.

To make the deviled eggs: Coarsely grate 1 whole egg and put in a medium bowl. Cut the remaining 6 in half evenly and, using a teaspoon, carefully remove the yolks and put in a small bowl. Grate the yolks into the medium bowl with the grated whole egg. Mash with a fork and add the sugar, mustard, mayonnaise, relish, and red onion. Season with salt and pepper. Add a little more mayonnaise if necessary. Using a spoon, mound the yolk filling into the 12 empty egg halves.

In a large bowl, toss the greens with the vinaigrette and a little extra salt and pepper.

Divide the dressed greens among 6 plates.

Place 2 deviled egg halves on the side of each plate, and sprinkle the eggs with a little paprika.

KITCHEN TIP
This vinaigrette is delicious for basting a turkey or chicken, and the drippings make a fabulous gravy.

PICKLED CAULIFLOWER

I planted enough cauliflower in my winter garden to feed the neighborhood. By the end of the season, with three or four gigantic heads still staring me in the face, I decided to make these delicious cauliflower pickles.

1 large head cauliflower (about 3 pounds), cut into florets

4 garlic cloves, smashed

1 jalapeño chile pepper, quartered and seeded

6 whole peppercorns

2 bay leaves

5 cups rice vinegar

Pour 1 inch of water into a large saucepan over high heat. Place a steamer basket in the pan and bring to a boil. Put the cauliflower in the basket and steam for 4 minutes, or until tender-crisp. Transfer to a colander and run under cold water. Drain completely.

While the cauliflower cooks, divide the garlic, chile pepper, peppercorns, and bay leaves between two 2-quart jars. Add the cauliflower and completely cover with vinegar. Cover and refrigerate for at least 2 days and up to 3 weeks. Remove and discard the bay leaves before serving.

PUMPKIN-RAISIN BREAD PUDDING

MAKES
10
SERVINGS

Vanilla ice cream or warm vanilla custard are dreamy with this hearty dessert. But I really like it best the next day for breakfast with a cup of steaming hot English Breakfast tea.

1 medium, wide-based, short pumpkin (about 2 to 3 pounds)

6 tablespoons unsalted butter, melted

¾ cup packed brown sugar

1 teaspoon ground cinnamon

¼ cup pure maple syrup

1 loaf (¾ pound) dense white bread, such as Italian, challah, or English muffin bread

¾ cup golden raisins

½ cup chopped walnuts or pecans

1½ cups whole milk or half-and-half

3 large eggs

Preheat the oven to 375°F. Cut the top off the pumpkin. Clean out the seeds and scrape out the stringy membranes, and discard.

In a small bowl, combine the butter, brown sugar, cinnamon, and maple syrup. Brush the inside of the pumpkin with 1 tablespoon of the butter mixture. Place on a baking sheet and bake for 45 minutes, or until tender when pierced with a fork.

Meanwhile, break the bread into bite-size pieces and put in a large bowl with the raisins and nuts. Pour the remaining butter mixture over the bread and toss to coat well.

In a measuring cup, whisk together the milk or half-and-half and eggs.

When the pumpkin is tender, remove it from the oven and carefully fill it with the bread mixture. Top with the egg mixture. Push the ingredients down so that everything is soaked in the liquid.

Return to the oven and bake for 1 hour, or until the pudding puffs up in the middle and a knife inserted near the center comes out clean. Place on a rack and cool for at least 30 minutes. Cut into wedges to serve.

AUTUMN FRUIT CRISP
WITH CRANBERRIES

Apples, pears, Fuyu persimmons—any hearty autumn fruit is great in this recipe. The cranberries add tartness and color.

Topping

2 cups whole grain pastry flour

2 cups rolled oats

2 teaspoons ground cinnamon

½ teaspoon ground cloves

½ cup (1 stick) unsalted butter, softened slightly and cut into pieces

Fruit Mixture

8 to 10 pears, apples, or Fuyu persimmons, peeled and cut into thin wedges

1½ cups fresh or frozen cranberries

1 cup sugar

3 tablespoons unsalted butter

Preheat the oven to 350°F. Butter a 3-quart baking dish.

To make the topping: In a medium bowl, combine the flour, oats, cinnamon, and cloves. Using your hands or a pastry blender, work the butter into the flour mixture until the pieces are about the size of peas.

To make the fruit mixture: In a large bowl, combine the cut-up fruit, cranberries, and sugar. Transfer to the prepared baking dish. Cut the butter into small pieces and sprinkle evenly over the fruit mixture.

Crumble the oat topping over the fruit. Bake for 40 minutes, or until the fruit is soft and the topping is lightly browned.

ORGANIC TIP

To keep this crisp true to the spirit of this book, use whatever seasonal organic fruits are available. In spring, cherries and apricots are wonderful; in summer, use berries and peaches; and in the dark of winter, consider plumping up dried fruits along with some fresh apples for a hearty crisp. The topping stays the same.

APPLE-ASIAGO PIE

This recipe, which was developed by a former pastry chef at Flea St. Café, remains my son's favorite version of apple pie. A twist on the classic combination of Cheddar cheese and apples, it may sound a bit unusual, but to us it's even better.

Crust

1½ cups whole grain pastry flour

1½ teaspoons dried thyme

¼ teaspoon salt

½ cup (1 stick) cold unsalted butter

½ cup milk

Topping

1 cup whole grain pastry flour

1 cup packed brown sugar

1 cup grated Asiago cheese (about 4 ounces)

½ teaspoon freshly ground black pepper

6 tablespoons cold unsalted butter

Filling

6 large crisp apples, such as Granny Smith, Crispin, or Gala, peeled, cored, and thinly sliced

¾ cup packed brown sugar

1 tablespoon cornstarch

¼ teaspoon freshly grated nutmeg

To make the crust: In a large bowl, combine the flour, thyme, and salt. Grate the butter into the mixture. Using your hands or a pastry blender, work the butter into the flour mixture until the pieces are about the size of peas. Add the milk, ¼ cup at a time, and blend until a soft, moist dough is formed. Add a few more tablespoons of milk if the dough seems dry. It should be somewhat sticky.

Form the dough into a ball, then flatten into a round disk. Wrap in plastic wrap and refrigerate for at least 1 hour.

To make the topping: In a medium bowl, combine the flour, brown sugar, cheese, and pepper. Grate the butter into the mixture. Using your hands or a pastry blender, work the butter into the flour mixture until the pieces are about the size of peas. Refrigerate until ready to use.

Preheat the oven to 350°F. When the piecrust dough is chilled, place it on a well-floured surface and roll to about a ⅛-inch thickness, turning and flouring the dough often to keep it from sticking. Fold the dough in half and place in a 9- or 10-inch pie plate. Unfold the dough, turn under the edges, and crimp them.

To make the filling: In a large bowl, combine the apples, brown sugar, cornstarch, and nutmeg. Transfer to the prepared crust.

Crumble the crumb topping over the apples. Bake for 1 hour, or until the crust is browned and the apples are soft. Place on a rack to cool for at least 30 minutes before slicing.

MY FAVORITE NUT PIE

My family always enjoys a gooey nut pie, and somehow, it seems to disappear by the sliver. Organic nuts are more widely available now, and a combination of them is what makes this pie unique. I don't like to refrigerate it because I prefer the taste at room temperature.

Crust

1 cup whole grain pastry flour

1 teaspoon sugar

½ teaspoon salt

½ cup (1 stick) cold unsalted butter

1 teaspoon red wine vinegar

½ cup ice water

Filling

2 tablespoons unsalted butter, softened

½ cup packed brown sugar

1 cup light corn syrup

3 large eggs

1½ teaspoons cornstarch

2 teaspoons vanilla extract

1½ cups mixed nuts, such as pistachios, walnuts, pecans, pine nuts, almonds, cashews, and hazelnuts, coarsely chopped

To make the crust: In a large bowl, combine the flour, sugar, and salt. Grate the butter into the mixture. Using your hands or a pastry blender, work the butter into the flour mixture until the pieces are about the size of peas.

In a small bowl, combine the vinegar and water. Add to the flour mixture, 1 tablespoon at a time, and blend until a soft, moist dough is formed. It should be somewhat sticky.

Form the dough into a ball, then flatten into a round disk. Wrap in plastic wrap and refrigerate for at least 1 hour.

When the dough is chilled, place it on a well-floured surface and roll to about a ⅛-inch thickness, turning and flouring the dough often

to keep it from sticking. Fold the dough in half and place in a 9- or 10-inch pie plate. Unfold the dough, turn under the edges, and crimp them. Refrigerate while you make the filling.

Preheat the oven to 375°F.

To make the filling: In a large bowl, with an electric mixer on medium speed, beat the butter, brown sugar, and corn syrup until well blended. Add the eggs, cornstarch, and vanilla extract and beat until smooth.

Scatter the nuts on the bottom of the chilled pie crust. Top with the egg mixture. Bake for 45 minutes, or until a knife inserted near the center comes out clean. Cool completely before serving.

FROG'S LEAP WINERY

About the time I was opening my first restaurant, John Williams sold his motorcycle to start Frog's Leap Winery. Ever since, it seems as though we have been on parallel tracks.

It's difficult to say enough about the delicious wines of Frog's Leap Winery. Over the twenty-five years I have had them on one wine list or another, they have always delivered great pleasure to my guests (and I must admit I have popped a few of their famous "Ribbit" corks for my own research).

Be it the crisp, lively Sauvignon Blanc, the wonderful non-Californian–style Chardonnay, the lip-smacking Zinfandel, or their classic Merlots and Cabernets, Frog's Leap wines always go well with whatever I'm cooking. Actually, though, it's when you look beyond the great wines and the iconoclastic labels that you start to discover even more to like about Frog's Leap.

First of all, and perhaps closest to my heart, Frog's Leap Winery was the first winery in the Napa Valley to commit to growing its grapes organically, certifying its first vineyards in 1988. Frog's Leap has gone beyond farming its own two hundred acres organically. Working with my dear friend "Amigo" Bob Cantisano, it has also mentored many other Napa Valley growers who are now following suit.

Frog's Leap farms all its vineyards without irrigation. Less than thirty years ago, nearly all vineyards in Napa were dry-farmed. Now it is exceedingly rare. John, Frog's Leap's owner and winemaker, explains that growing grapes without irrigation forces the vines to sink their roots more deeply into the ground to get water. Frog's Leap's grapes have deep natural flavors with great balance and finesse, and the resulting wines deliver great flavors at lower alcohol levels—something that my diners appreciate.

A visit to Frog's Leap is a sensory and ecological delight. One always leaves the acres of gardens and orchards (all organic, of course) that supplement its vineyards with a few garden goodies under the arm.

Frog's Leap has also been an early advocate of socially responsible business. Its winery is entirely solar powered, its offices are heated and cooled with geothermal energy, and its newly constructed buildings meet LEED (Leadership in Energy and Environmental Design) standards, the ultimate badge of green building. Frog's Leap has also shown leadership in everything from river restoration to socially responsible farmworker employment. It is an example of how business can make a difference while making a profit.

Last, but not least, I have to say this about Frog's Leap: These people know how to have fun! In addition, they seem eager to have you and me join in. From their Ribbit cork to the dire warning at the bottom of every bottle ("Open other end"), their sense of humor and sheer joy in life show through everything they do. I hope you get to know Frog's Leap as I have over the years. You won't regret it.

EARLY WINTER

My cooking is always at its best during the winter months. Even though I live in Northern California, winter still brings back memories of the days when I lived in a rural town in central Maine. Winters there were stubbornly long. The lake within view of my front yard sometimes didn't thaw until May. Summers quickly came and went. It was there that I really learned about winter cooking. | During the shorter days of winter, I tend to spend more time at home, watching videos, folding laundry, or in other homey activities while a pot of goodness simmers on my kitchen stove. I rely on more canned, dried, and frozen organic foods. I prepare a lot of savory, slow-cooked dishes made with grains and pastas, and use more spices and heartier herbs. Winter cooking can fill a house for hours with wonderful aromas that waft and dance from room to room and warm me like a favorite throw blanket or thick wool sweater. Since there is less fresh food available, I honor anything that I can get my hands on. Winter foods may not be as bright and light as summer crops, but they provide soulful comfort. | At this time of the year, nurturing and hearty meals are savored. During cold months, we naturally hunger for dishes that fill our bellies with warmth and satisfaction and provide the energy we need.

PEAR, BRIE, AND OLIVE TART

MAKES
8
SERVINGS

One bite of the crisp sweetness of the pear, the saltiness of the olive, and the creaminess of the Brie is unforgettable. This tart works both as an appetizer with champagne or as a dessert with ruby port.

Crust

1 cup unbleached all-purpose flour

¼ cup very finely ground walnuts

½ teaspoon salt

½ teaspoon freshly ground black pepper

½ cup (1 stick) cold unsalted butter

½ cup ice water

Filling

1 red onion, thinly sliced

2 pears, cored and thinly sliced

2 tablespoons sugar

2 teaspoons chopped fresh thyme

4 ounces Brie cheese, cut into small pieces

½ cup kalamata olives, pitted and halved

To make the crust: In a large bowl, combine the flour, walnuts, salt, and pepper. Grate the butter into the mixture. Using your hands or a pastry blender, work the butter into the flour mixture until the pieces are about the size of peas.

Add the water, 1 tablespoon at a time, and blend until you have a soft, moist dough. Form the dough into a ball, then flatten into a round disk. Wrap in plastic wrap and refrigerate for at least 1 hour.

Preheat the oven to 400°F. Line a baking sheet with parchment paper

On a well-floured board, roll the dough into a ⅛-inch-thick oval. Fold the dough in half crosswise and place in the center of the prepared baking sheet. Unfold the dough. The edges will fall over the sides of the baking sheet.

To make the filling: Arrange the onion in the center of the crust, leaving a 1½- to 2-inch border. Arrange the pears on top and sprinkle with the sugar and thyme. Top with the Brie and olives. Using your fingers, roll under the edges of the dough to form a pastry shell and crimp the edges.

Bake for 20 to 30 minutes, or until the crust is golden brown.

KITCHEN TIP

Another way to prepare this free-form tart is to bake it on a pizza stone. Or, for a more formal tart, shape the dough in a tart pan.

GNOCCHI WITH SAGE BUTTER

Sometimes, to add interest, I substitute sweet potatoes for the russets or stir in an herb or spice or even some grated hard cheese. Once you have mastered the technique, be adventurous and add your own flavor enhancers.

Gnocchi

2 large russet potatoes (about 1½ pounds)

1 large egg, beaten

1 teaspoon salt

½ to 1 cup unbleached all-purpose flour

Sauce

3 tablespoons unsalted butter

1 shallot, minced

1 garlic clove, minced

3 tablespoons chopped fresh sage

¼ cup minced fresh Italian parsley

¼ cup dry vermouth

Salt

Freshly ground black pepper

¼ cup grated Romano cheese (about 1 ounce)

Preheat the oven to 450°F.

To make the gnocchi: Pierce the potatoes a couple of times so that the steam can escape, and bake for 50 to 65 minutes, or until very soft. Remove and set aside until cool enough to handle.

Bring a large pot of water to a boil over high heat. Cut the potatoes in half, scoop out the flesh, and discard the skins. Push the flesh through a potato ricer or mash thoroughly with a fork and transfer to a large bowl. Stir in the egg and salt.

Add the flour, ¼ cup at a time, using your hands and blending just until the dough holds together. Pinch off 1 teaspoon of the dough and roll into a ball on a floured surface. Drop into the boiling water. If the piece falls apart, add more flour to the dough, 2 tablespoons at a time. Repeat the cooking test, adding more flour if necessary, until the gnocchi holds together and floats to the surface.

Turn the dough out onto a well-floured board. Divide the dough into 5 pieces and roll each into a ¾-inch-thick rope. Be sure to roll the ropes in flour to keep from sticking. Cut each rope into ¾-inch pieces. Lightly press each piece with a floured fork or thumb and make a slight indention. Dust the gnocchi with flour. If not cooking right away, place on a baking pan, cover, and refrigerate or freeze until ready to cook.

To cook the gnocchi, add salt to the boiling water and drop the gnocchi in. Cook until they rise to the surface. Remove with a slotted spoon to a colander.

To make the sauce: Melt the butter in a medium saucepan over medium heat. Add the shallot, garlic, and sage and cook for 4 minutes, or until lightly browned. Add the parsley and vermouth. Season with salt and pepper to taste. Transfer the gnocchi to a serving bowl and top with the sauce and cheese.

KITCHEN TIP
To make gnocchi light and fluffy, use as little flour as possible, just so they hold together; too much makes them heavy.

CHARD AND FETA PIE

Serve a sliver of this pie as an interesting alternative to potatoes with meat or fish. Or, for a light supper, serve a larger slice with a salad and warm bread.

2 cups shredded potatoes, such as red-skinned, Yellow Finn, or Bintjes (about 2 large)

2 green onions, minced

¾ teaspoon salt

6 large eggs

¼ cup unbleached all-purpose flour

¼ teaspoon freshly ground black pepper

2 tablespoons olive oil

1 red onion, finely chopped

2 garlic cloves, minced

2 bunches green or red chard or spinach, coarsely chopped

1½ cups crumbled feta cheese (about 8 ounces)

1 cup milk

2 tablespoons chopped fresh oregano

½ cup dry bread crumbs

Preheat the oven to 400°F. Lightly oil a 9-inch deep-dish pie plate.

Put the potatoes and green onions in a colander and sprinkle with ½ teaspoon of the salt. Drain for 5 minutes, gently squeezing out any excess liquid.

Transfer to a medium bowl and add 1 of the eggs, the flour, and pepper. Stir until well blended. Press into the prepared pie plate to form a crust. Brush with 1 tablespoon of the oil. Bake for 30 minutes, or until the crust is browned.

Meanwhile, heat the remaining 1 tablespoon oil in a medium skillet over medium-high heat. Add the red onion and cook for 4 minutes, or until soft. Add the garlic and chard or spinach and cook, stirring often, for 3 minutes, or until the chard or spinach is wilted. Remove from the heat, drain off excess liquid, and cool slightly.

In a large bowl, combine the remaining 5 eggs, 1 cup of the cheese, the milk, oregano, the remaining ¼ teaspoon salt, and the chard mixture. Pour into the baked crust. Sprinkle the top with the bread crumbs and the remaining ½ cup cheese.

Reduce the heat to 350°F. Bake for 35 minutes, or until a knife inserted in the center comes out clean. Let stand for 15 minutes before cutting.

SEAFOOD AND ANGEL HAIR PASTA

Rich, tender seafood marries beautifully with thin strands of pasta, tender chard, and a creamy tomato sauce.

1 lobster tail (about 1 pound)

2 tablespoons unsalted butter

2 tablespoons olive oil

4 to 6 garlic cloves, minced

2 shallots, thinly sliced

1 can (14½ ounces) diced tomatoes
    with their juice

1 cup clam juice or chicken broth

½ cup dry vermouth

1 tablespoon chopped fresh thyme

1 teaspoon paprika

2 teaspoons grated lime zest

1 cup heavy cream (optional)

1 pound clams, such as littleneck,
    Manila, or cherrystone, scrubbed

Salt

Freshly ground black pepper

Pinch of ground red (cayenne) or
    chipotle pepper (optional)

12 ounces angel hair pasta

1 pound chard, tougher, large stems
    removed and discarded

Cut down the belly side of the lobster tail and remove the meat. Remove all fibrous or dark-colored membranes and cut the meat into bite-size pieces. Refrigerate until ready to use.

Cut the lobster shell into 4 pieces.

Heat the butter and oil in a large saucepan over medium-high heat. Add the garlic and shallots and cook for 2 minutes. Add the tomatoes with juice, clam juice or broth, vermouth, and the lobster shells. Bring to a boil. Reduce the heat to low, cover, and simmer for 15 minutes.

Remove and discard the lobster shells. Add the thyme, paprika, lime zest, and cream, if using. Cook, uncovered, for 20 minutes, or until reduced by one-third. Bring a large pot of water to a boil for the pasta.

Add the lobster meat and clams to the sauce. Season to taste with the salt, black pepper, and red or chipotle pepper. Cover and simmer for 3 to 5 minutes, or until the clams open and the lobster turns opaque. Discard any unopened clams.

While the seafood is simmering, cook the pasta according to package directions, adding the chard during the last minute of cooking time. Drain and place in a large bowl. Pour the seafood sauce over the pasta and chard.

VARIATION
If you don't want to bother with lobster, substitute ¾ pound shrimp or scallops.

CORNMEAL-CRUSTED COD WITH GARLICKY TATSOI

The combination of cod, cornmeal, and tatsoi in this recipe is wonderful. A few drops of hot sauce can really pull it all together. You will need about six ounces or two heads of tatsoi per person, to allow for shrinkage when it cooks. If you can't find tatsoi, spinach is the perfect substitute.

4 cod or scrod fillets (about 4 ounces each)

1½ cups buttermilk (see Organic Tip on page 38)

1 cup cornmeal

3 tablespoons chopped fresh Italian parsley

1 tablespoon dried oregano

2 teaspoons dried thyme

1½ teaspoons salt

½ teaspoon freshly ground black pepper

¼ to 1 teaspoon ground red pepper (cayenne)

4 tablespoons olive oil

2 garlic cloves, minced

1½ pounds tatsoi, steamed lightly

Juice and grated zest of 1 lemon

1 tablespoon soy sauce

The night before serving, put the fillets in a bowl and pour the buttermilk over all. Toss to coat. Cover and refrigerate.

Preheat the oven to 250°F.

In a pie plate, combine the cornmeal, parsley, oregano, thyme, salt, black pepper, and ground red pepper. Remove the fish from the buttermilk, shaking off any excess. Dip the fish in the cornmeal mixture, turning to coat completely.

Heat 1½ tablespoons of the oil in a large skillet over medium heat. Add 2 fillets and cook for 8 to 10 minutes, turning once, or until browned and the fish flakes easily. Place on a baking sheet and keep warm in the oven. Repeat with 1½ tablespoons more oil and the remaining 2 fillets.

Wipe the skillet clean and heat the remaining 1 tablespoon oil over medium heat. Add the garlic and cook for 2 minutes. Add the tatsoi, lemon juice, and soy sauce and cook for 3 minutes, or until heated through. Transfer to a serving platter and top with the fillets. Sprinkle with the lemon zest.

ROAST CHICKEN WITH MASHED CELERY ROOT AND POTATOES

MAKES

6

SERVINGS

You can use any cut of chicken for this dish, but my preference is to roast a whole one. I like serving it family style, with the whole roast chicken perched on top of the mashed celery root and potatoes. Drizzle any pan juices from the chicken over everything as a sauce *au naturel!* Round out the meal with steamed vegetables, such as broccoli, kale, or Brussels sprouts, tossed with a little olive oil and garlic.

1 teaspoon ground cumin

1 teaspoon paprika

½ teaspoon salt

½ teaspoon freshly ground black pepper

1 roasting chicken (3 to 4 pounds)

2 tablespoons olive oil

1 large onion, thinly sliced

1 pound celery root, peeled and cut into wedges

8 ounces potatoes, peeled and cut into wedges

¼ cup chicken broth or milk

Salt

Freshly ground black pepper

2 tablespoons chopped fresh Italian parsley

Preheat the oven to 475°F.

In a small bowl, combine the cumin, paprika, salt, and pepper. Put the chicken on a rack in a large roasting pan. Rub half of the cumin mixture over the chicken and season the inside of the chicken with the rest of it. Roast for 20 minutes. Reduce the heat to 375°F and continue roasting for 1 to 1¼ hours, or until a thermometer inserted in a breast registers 180°F and the juices run clear. Let stand for 10 minutes before carving.

Meanwhile, heat the oil in a medium skillet over medium heat. Add the onion, cover, and cook for 6 minutes, or until very soft.

Bring a large pot of salted water to a boil. Add the celery root and potatoes and cook for 15 minutes, or until tender. Drain and transfer to a large bowl. Mash the potatoes and celery root, adding enough broth or milk so they are creamy. Stir in the onion and season with salt and pepper to taste.

Spoon all the mashed vegetables onto a large serving platter. Remove the chicken from the oven and place on the vegetables.

Skim the fat off the pan juices and pour the juices over the chicken and vegetables. Sprinkle with the parsley.

GAME HEN WITH AROMATIC SWEET POTATOES AND PRUNES

This aromatic dish is even better when served the next day. It is similar to *tsimmis,* a recipe from my childhood that my mom made on Rosh Hashanah, the Jewish New Year. The combination of the sweet potatoes and dried fruit symbolizes a wish for sweetness in the new year, which somehow made this dish taste even better to me. Chicken, or even rabbit, would be a fine substitute for the game hen.

1½ pounds sweet potatoes, peeled and cubed

1 large onion, thinly sliced

2 tablespoons olive oil

1 teaspoon ground turmeric

1 teaspoon paprika

1 teaspoon ground coriander

¼ teaspoon salt

¼ teaspoon freshly ground black pepper

4 small game hens

2 cups chicken broth

3 tablespoons brown sugar

2 teaspoons ground cinnamon

1½ cups pitted prunes

½ cup canned chickpeas, rinsed and drained

¼ cup chopped fresh cilantro

Pinch of saffron (optional)

Preheat the oven to 400°F.

In a large, deep roasting pan, toss the sweet potatoes and onion with 1 tablespoon of the oil.

In a small bowl, combine the turmeric, paprika, coriander, salt, and pepper.

Rub the hens with the remaining 1 tablespoon oil and generously sprinkle with the spice mixture. Place the hens on the sweet potatoes and roast for 30 minutes.

In a medium saucepan, combine the broth, brown sugar, cinnamon, prunes, chickpeas, cilantro, and saffron, if using. Bring to a boil over high heat.

Remove the baking dish from the oven and pour the prune mixture over the potatoes, stirring to blend. Reduce the heat to 350°F. Roast, stirring the potatoes occasionally, for 45 to 55 minutes, or until a thermometer inserted in a breast registers 180°F and the juices run clear. Let stand for 10 minutes before serving.

SWEET-AND-SOUR CABBAGE WITH SMOKED PORK CHOPS

MAKES

4

SERVINGS

This dish is one of my all-time favorites. Slow-cooking cabbage and onion brings out a mellow, soft flavor that is further enhanced by a touch of brown sugar and vinegar. The cabbage is wonderful with smoked meats.

1 tablespoon olive oil

1 head cabbage, cored and very thinly sliced (about 6 cups)

1 red onion, thinly sliced

½ cup packed brown sugar

½ cup rice wine vinegar

Salt

Freshly ground black pepper

4 smoked pork chops (about 5 ounces each)

¼ cup Dijon mustard

1 tablespoon honey

Heat the oil in a Dutch oven over medium heat. Add the cabbage and onion and cook, stirring, for 2 minutes. Reduce the heat to low, cover, and cook, stirring often, for 45 minutes, or until very soft. Add the brown sugar and vinegar and cook for 5 minutes. Season with salt and pepper to taste. Place the chops on top of the cabbage.

Cover and cook for 20 minutes, or until the chops are heated through.

Meanwhile, in a small bowl, combine the mustard and honey.

Remove the cabbage mixture to a large platter and top with the chops. Drizzle the mustard mixture over the chops.

POT ROAST WITH WINTER VEGETABLES

MAKES

8

SERVINGS

Having gone through lean financial times, I have learned how to cook with cuts of meat that are less expensive and typically need slow cooking to tenderize them. Chuck or pot roast is a cut of beef that I love. Through hours of cooking over low heat, the meat becomes tender, absorbing the seasonings and flavors of the ingredients that are cooked alongside.

1 chuck or bottom round roast (about 3 pounds)

½ teaspoon salt

¼ teaspoon freshly ground black pepper

4 cups vegetable or beef broth

2 tablespoons Dijon mustard

10 large garlic cloves, chopped

2 tablespoons chopped fresh thyme

3 large sweet potatoes, peeled and cut into large chunks

3 large leeks (white part only), sliced and washed thoroughly

12 dried apricot halves, chopped

Preheat the oven to 500°F.

Put the roast in a large roasting pan and sprinkle with the salt and pepper. Roast for 45 minutes, turning once.

Meanwhile, in a large measuring cup, combine the broth, mustard, garlic, and thyme.

Reduce the heat to 350°F. Pour the broth mixture over the meat, cover, and roast for 1 hour.

Add the sweet potatoes, leeks, and apricots. Roast for 2 hours, or until the meat is falling-apart tender when tested with a fork. Using tongs or a large spoon and fork, remove the roast to a cutting board. Slice or, with a fork, pull away pieces. Spoon the sweet potato mixture onto a platter or individual plates. Top with the meat and drizzle with juices from the pan.

ROASTED RUTABAGA
WITH LAMB SAUSAGE

MAKES

6

SERVINGS

When oven-roasted, rutabagas turn golden and creamy. This dish reminds me of food that one might find in a country pub in northern England. If you can't find lamb sausage, pork or chicken will work just as well.

2 pounds lamb sausage

1 large rutabaga (about ¾ pound), peeled and cut into thick wedges

1 large red onion, sliced

3 to 4 garlic cloves, minced

1 tablespoon chopped fresh rosemary

½ cup blackberry or raspberry preserves

2 to 3 tablespoons balsamic vinegar

Salt

Freshly ground black pepper

Preheat the oven to 500°F. Put the sausage in a large shallow roasting pan. Cook, turning occasionally, for 15 minutes.

Reduce the temperature to 350°F. Remove the sausage to a plate. Add the rutabaga, onion, garlic, rosemary, and preserves to the pan with the sausage drippings. Toss to coat well. Place the sausage on top of the vegetables. Cover and roast, tossing occasionally, for 45 minutes, or until the vegetables are tender and the sausage is cooked through.

Transfer the sausage to a platter. Drizzle the vinegar over the vegetables. Mix well and season with salt and pepper to taste. Serve with the sausage.

BROCCOLI WITH CASHEWS

Broccoli is a vegetable that can almost always be found in the organic section of the produce department. It holds up well when stored, but when it is fresh—just picked from the garden or bought at a farmers' market—the sweet, earthy flavors are remarkably different.

This is one of the most popular salads in our deli case at jZcool and one that I reach for more often than any other.

1 large bunch broccoli

⅓ cup mayonnaise

3 tablespoons red wine vinegar

2 tablespoons brown sugar

½ medium red onion, very thinly sliced

½ cup cashews

¼ cup raisins

Salt

Freshly ground black pepper

Cut the broccoli top into florets. Peel away the fibrous skin from the thick stems, and thinly slice. Place a large bowl of ice water on the counter near the stove. Place a large pot of water over high heat and bring to a boil. Add the broccoli and blanch for about 3 to 5 minutes, or until bright green and tender-crisp. Meanwhile, in a large mixing bowl, mix together the mayonnaise, vinegar, sugar, and red onion.

When the broccoli feels tender when tested with the tip of a knife, drain and plunge into the ice water. Drain again and transfer to the bowl with the dressing. Add the cashews and raisins. Mix well and season with salt and pepper.

ORANGES, BEETS, AND OLIVES

The combination of sweet beets and tangy oranges is taken to a higher level with the addition of salty olives and zesty chives.

6 beets, trimmed and scrubbed

Juice of 2 blood oranges

½ cup kalamata olives, pitted

3 tablespoons balsamic vinegar

2 tablespoons extra-virgin olive oil

2 tablespoons grated fresh ginger

2 tablespoons chopped fresh chives

Salt

Put the beets in a medium saucepan and cover with water. Bring to a boil over high heat. Reduce the heat to low, cover, and simmer for 45 minutes, or until the beets are tender.

Drain the beets and run under cold water to remove the skins. Cut the beets into ¼-inch cubes and transfer to a large bowl.

Squeeze the juice from the oranges and pour over the beets. Add the olives, vinegar, oil, ginger, and chives. Toss to coat well and let sit for 5 minutes. Season with salt to taste.

KITCHEN TIP
If you can't find blood oranges, use ½ cup orange juice instead.

HONEY-GLAZED CARROTS

6

SERVINGS

The aroma and flavor of these carrots are enticing. I like them with roasted lamb, served along with saffron-scented rice or couscous.

1 tablespoon unsalted butter

1 leek (white part only), halved lengthwise, sliced, and washed thoroughly

1 pound carrots, sliced

1 cup apple juice

¼ cup honey

1 cinnamon stick

1 teaspoon ground cumin

2 teaspoons chopped fresh mint

¼ teaspoon salt

Melt the butter in a medium saucepan over medium-high heat. Add the leek and cook for 2 minutes, or until lightly browned. Add the carrots and cook for 2 minutes, or until lightly browned. Add the apple juice, honey, cinnamon stick, cumin, mint, and salt and bring to a boil. Reduce the heat to low, cover, and simmer for 15 minutes, or until the carrots are very soft. Remove and discard the cinnamon stick before serving.

VARIATION

This honey sauce is terrific with frozen vegetables, too. Replace the carrots with a bag of frozen peas and carrots, but add the frozen vegetables after cooking the sauce for 10 minutes.

KALE SALAD

This recipe was inspired by one of my favorite farmers and dearest friends, Stuart Dickson. He is an amazing cook and farmer and has taught me much about cooking. Did I mention that my farmer friends are the ones who have taught me to cook? They know so much about the food they grow and put in our hands. Often, I find inspiration in their simple descriptions of how they like to eat what they have grown. Stuart loves kale, and this is one of his favorite ways to eat it.

1 large bunch kale, thinly sliced

¼ cup extra-virgin olive oil

1 small red onion, thinly sliced

2 garlic cloves, minced

3 tablespoons balsamic vinegar

1 hot chile pepper, such as jalapeño, serrano, or habanero, seeded and minced

Salt

Freshly ground black pepper

Put the kale in a large serving bowl; set aside at room temperature.

Heat the oil in a small saucepan over medium-low heat. Add the onion and garlic and cook for 6 minutes, or until very soft. Add the vinegar and chile pepper. Cook for 1 minute. Pour the mixture over the kale and toss well. Season with salt and black pepper to taste and serve immediately.

VARIATION

I love this salad with bits of soft goat cheese crumbled over the top.

WINTER GREENS AND EGG SALAD

This is one of my favorite salads. It was inspired by my grandfather, who used to pick wild dandelions from our neighbors' yards. A bold, fruity olive oil and good-quality red wine vinegar are key to the success of this robust salad.

¼ cup extra-virgin olive oil

3 tablespoons red wine vinegar

1 tablespoon brown sugar

1 to 2 garlic cloves, thinly sliced

¼ teaspoon salt

¼ teaspoon freshly ground black pepper

1 pound bitter greens, such as frisée, radicchio, endive, or dandelion, torn into bite-size pieces

2 green onions, thinly sliced

3 hard-cooked large eggs, peeled and chopped

1 tablespoon capers

In a large bowl, whisk together the oil, vinegar, sugar, garlic, salt, and pepper. Add the greens and green onions and toss to coat well. Top with the eggs and capers and serve.

KITCHEN TIP

This is one salad that is still good the next day. I like it tucked into sandwiches, along with salty meats or pungent cheeses.

GINGERBREAD FRUITCAKE

You either love fruitcake or you don't. I find that it is the candied fruit that turns people away. In this recipe, dried organic fruit is used instead of the usual sugary, artificially colored fruit. The gingery cake celebrates the holiday season and is almost too good to call fruitcake.

1⅓ cups unbleached all-purpose flour

1 teaspoon baking powder

1 teaspoon ground cinnamon

1 teaspoon ground ginger

¾ teaspoon freshly ground black pepper

¾ teaspoon ground allspice

½ teaspoon baking soda

½ teaspoon salt

⅓ cup unsalted butter, softened

½ cup packed brown sugar or honey

½ cup molasses

1 large egg, beaten

¾ cup buttermilk (see Organic Tip on page 38)

1 teaspoon vanilla extract

1½ cups dried fruit, such as apricots, peaches, cherries, cranberries, figs, dates, and/or apples, finely chopped

½ cup chopped walnuts or pecans

Preheat the oven to 375°F. Lightly butter a 10-inch springform pan.

In a medium bowl, combine the flour, baking powder, cinnamon, ginger, pepper, allspice, baking soda, and salt. Set aside.

In a large bowl, with an electric mixer on medium speed, beat the butter and brown sugar or honey until creamy. Beat in the molasses, egg, buttermilk, and vanilla extract.

On low speed, gradually beat in the flour mixture just until blended. Stir in the dried fruit and nuts.

Pour the batter into the prepared pan and bake for 35 minutes, or until a wooden pick inserted in the center comes out clean. Cool in the pan on a rack for 30 minutes. Remove the sides from the pan. Transfer the cake to a serving plate and serve warm, or cool completely and serve.

KITCHEN TIPS

This cake screams for ice cream. At this time of the year, you might find pumpkin ice cream, which would be wonderful. Otherwise, go with pure vanilla or honey-vanilla.

Make individual fruitcakes in muffin tins (bake for 15 to 20 minutes) and serve with warm homemade custard for a spectacular holiday treat.

MIRIN-BAKED PEARS

This light and pleasant dessert is wonderful with ginger cookies or over vanilla ice cream. *Shiso* is an herb that is used frequently in Japanese cooking, but rarely for dessert. It adds a subtle, minty interest to the poached pears. If you can't find it, use fresh mint.

6 small pears, peeled, cored, and halved

2 cups mirin cooking wine

½ cup sugar

6 whole cloves

2 tablespoons finely chopped crystallized ginger

3 tablespoons thinly sliced fresh *shiso* or mint

Preheat the oven to 375°F.

Place the pears, cut side down, in a 9-inch square baking dish.

In a large measuring cup, combine the mirin, sugar, cloves, and ginger. Pour over the pears.

Bake, basting every 10 minutes, for 45 minutes, or until the pears are tender. Remove from the oven and sprinkle with the *shiso* or mint. Serve warm or refrigerate and serve cold.

ORANGE-MINT GRANITA

This simple frozen dessert is quite refreshing, and it can also be served between courses. If you can find them, use blood oranges for the orange juice. They'll give the sorbet extraordinary color.

1 cup sugar

1 cup water

3 cups cold freshly squeezed orange juice

¼ cup chopped fresh mint

Place a 9-inch square metal baking pan in the freezer.

In a small saucepan over medium-high heat, bring the sugar and water to a boil and continue boiling for 5 minutes. Transfer to a large bowl and cool completely.

When cooled, add the orange juice and mint. Pour into the frozen baking pan, cover with foil, and return to the freezer. Freeze, stirring occasionally, for 3 hours, or until partially frozen.

Transfer the mixture to a food processor and process until smooth, but still frozen. Return the mixture to the pan, cover, and freeze for 3 hours longer, or until completely frozen.

Remove the sorbet from the freezer 15 minutes before serving and scoop into dessert bowls.

KITCHEN TIP

Granitas are smoothest when prepared in an ice-cream maker. If you have one, pour the orange mixture into the container of your ice-cream maker and prepare according to the manufacturer's directions.

SMALL PLANET FOODS

Small Planet Foods, the parent company for Cascadian and Muir Glen, was started by one of my heroes, Gene Kahn. Gene has gone from hippie organic farmer to showing large companies the many ways to approach sustainability. In our restaurants and when catering during the cold months, we use anything that is fresh and local. We also believe that preserved local organic ingredients are better than anything shipped from afar. Frozen vegetables and fruits from Cascadian, and Muir Glen's tomatoes, have long been mainstays in our winter organic pantry. We used them before they were available in grocery stores. In fact, in the late '70s, we actually had cans of Muir Glen tomatoes sent to us by UPS. Need I say more?

In 1972, Gene traveled west from Chicago in hope of a better life. He found a small farm in the shadow of the breathtaking North Cascade Mountains in northwest Washington state and began to follow his dream of organic farming. Today, Cascadian Farm is one of the top producers of organic food in the nation. Cascadian joined with Muir Glen in 1998 to create Small Planet Foods. The company's mission is to "provide great-tasting organic food that contributes to better health for our consumers and the planet."

Although there are many farms growing organic produce for the Cascadian Farm brand, there remains only one Cascadian home farm, where Gene Kahn started out decades ago. It is now a twenty-acre berry farm. The berries are cultivated with sustainable organic methods that protect the local ecosystem. Berries are harvested by hand, at the peak of ripeness and flavor. Then a small processing line sorts and packs them for the farm's roadside stand.

Muir Glen, Cascadian's sister company, is named after the legendary naturalist John Muir. The company was founded in 1991 by a group of entrepreneurs in the agricultural industry who were committed to encouraging farmers to grow tomatoes organically. All of Muir Glen's tomatoes are field-grown and vine-ripened under certified Organic practices—no synthetic pesticides, no chemical fertilizers, just gorgeous tomato taste, true to nature. From California's San Joaquin Valley, the heart of the country's prime tomato-growing region, Muir Glen produces its premium-quality organic tomato products, including canned tomatoes, salsa, ketchup, and soups.

DEEP WINTER

The heart of winter finds me in the kitchen wearing an oversized sweatshirt, baggy pants, and wool socks as I happily hum in front of my workhorse of a commercial gas stove. Strange as it sounds, this is my favorite time of the year to cook. It seems easier to plan when you have limited choices. I savor the challenge of working with a smaller variety of fresh foods and finding ways to prepare meals that keep warmth, comfort, and heartiness simmering on the front burner. | Of course, attempting to prepare Mediterranean foods during deep winter can be an undertaking. I remember a very cold, very stormy February when the farmers couldn't even get into their fields to harvest. The chef at my restaurant looked up at me and declared, "Jesse, there is simply nothing growing, and most of the produce kept in storage is downright gone." Somehow, we managed to produce wonderful braised, stewed, and roasted dishes that kept our customers' bellies full, warm, and happy. | Anyone can prepare for winter, even those who live in the coldest of climates. Think of deep winter as payoff time. I do. The Indian-summer nights I spent stacking fresh produce in my two food dryers are now reaping me rewards. Dried organic mushrooms, berries, figs, and tomatoes captured during their prime are ready for hearty dishes. | Enjoy these days. Spring is on its way.

WHITE BEANS, MUSTARD GREENS, AND ROASTED GARLIC BRUSCHETTA

This combination of white beans, garlic, and spicy mustard greens is not only full of calcium, but also jam-packed with flavor. There is nothing that compares with the creaminess of cooked dried white beans, but rinsed and drained canned beans work well in a pinch.

2 tablespoons olive oil

2 garlic cloves, minced

4 cups thickly sliced mustard greens

1 tablespoon balsamic vinegar

Salt

Freshly ground black pepper

½ red onion, minced

1 cup cooked white beans

2 teaspoons chopped fresh oregano

½ cup vegetable or chicken broth

6 slices (½ inch thick) Italian bread, toasted

Heat 1 tablespoon of the oil in a medium skillet over medium-low heat. Add the garlic and greens and cook for 5 minutes, or until the greens are very tender. Stir in the vinegar. Remove to a bowl and set aside to cool slightly. Season generously with salt and pepper to taste.

Heat the remaining 1 tablespoon oil in the same skillet over medium heat. Add the onion and cook for 5 minutes, or until soft. Add the beans, oregano, and broth. Cook for 5 minutes, or until heated through and well blended. Using a fork, mash the beans coarsely. Season with salt and pepper to taste.

Divide the greens evenly among the bread slices. Top each with an equal portion of the bean mixture. Serve immediately.

WINTER VEGETABLES WITH BAGNA CAUDA

This classic warm anchovy dip appeared often as an appetizer at my Italian grandfather's house. Just about any winter vegetable is wonderful with this warm, salty sauce, especially ones sweetened by the chill of frost, such as broccoli, turnips, beets, cauliflower, or carrots.

⅓ cup olive oil

4 tablespoons unsalted butter

3 cans (2 ounces each) anchovies packed in oil, drained

2 garlic cloves, thinly sliced

1½ teaspoons grated lemon zest

Pinch of red-pepper flakes (optional)

5 cups cut-up vegetables, such as broccoli, turnips, beets, cauliflower, and carrots, in bite-size pieces

1 fennel bulb, or 4 celery ribs, cut into 3-inch strips

In a medium saucepan over medium-high heat, bring the oil, butter, anchovies, garlic, and lemon zest to a boil. Reduce the heat to low and simmer for 5 minutes, or until the anchovies dissolve. Add the red-pepper flakes, if using. Transfer to a serving bowl.

Meanwhile, pour 1 inch of water into a large saucepan. Bring to a boil over high heat and insert a steamer basket or wire rack. Add the vegetables, reduce the heat to low, cover, and simmer for 8 minutes, or until the vegetables are tender. Remove and cool slightly. Place on a large serving platter with the fennel or celery. Serve with the sauce.

KITCHEN TIP

Bagna cauda is best served warm. I like to serve it in a butter warmer or a cast-iron skillet on a warming tray. Don't worry if there is some left over; simply store it in the refrigerator for up to a week, using small amounts to season vegetables or spoon over grilled fish.

BEET AND PARSNIP SOUP WITH DILL CREAM

The flavors and appearance of this passionately purple soup are balanced beautifully by the tart creaminess of the sour cream. At Flea St. Café we serve this soup on Valentine's Day, accompanied by heart-shaped biscuits.

6 cups vegetable or chicken broth

1 pound parsnips, cut into small cubes

6 beets, trimmed and scrubbed

1 large shallot, thinly sliced

3 whole cloves

3 whole peppercorns

3 tablespoons sugar

Salt

Freshly ground black pepper

1 cup sour cream or yogurt

1 green onion, finely chopped

2 tablespoons chopped fresh dill

Bring the broth to a boil in a large saucepan over high heat. Add the parsnips. Reduce the heat to low, cover, and simmer for 10 minutes, or until tender. Using a slotted spoon, remove the parsnips to a bowl.

Add the beets, shallot, cloves, and peppercorns to the simmering broth. Cover and simmer for 45 minutes, or until the beets are tender. Using a slotted spoon, remove the beets to the cutting board, reserving the liquid. When the beets are cool, slip off the skins. Cut into small cubes.

Strain the broth through a cheesecloth-lined sieve into a large bowl. Return the broth to the pot. Add the parsnips, beets, and sugar. Season to taste with salt and black pepper.

In a small bowl, combine the sour cream, green onion, and dill.

Ladle the soup into 6 bowls and top with the sour cream mixture.

WINTER SQUASH SOUP WITH DRIED FIGS AND TOASTED PINE NUTS

There is a wonderful selection of organic squash available throughout the winter. If you have the opportunity, try different varieties. With this soup, you will really be able to taste the subtle flavor quality in each. Winter squash soup is deeply satisfying and stick-to-the-ribs warming, and it is delicious with a hearty chicory salad.

2 tablespoons pine nuts

2 tablespoons olive oil

1 yellow onion, chopped coarsely

1 to 2 medium carrots, coarsely chopped

1 cup coarsely chopped fennel or celery

1/3 cup dry white wine

4 cups coarsely chopped peeled winter squash, such as butternut, acorn, hubbard, turban, or pumpkin

4 to 6 cups chicken or vegetable broth

2 tablespoons chopped fresh thyme

1/2 teaspoon ground coriander

1 teaspoon ground cinnamon

Salt

Freshly ground black pepper

1/2 cup coconut or cashew milk (optional; see Kitchen Tip)

Maple syrup

4 to 5 dried figs, cut into thin rounds

Put the pine nuts in a small, heavy-bottomed skillet over medium heat. Cook, shaking the skillet often, for 5 minutes, or until lightly browned and toasted.

In an 8-quart soup pot, over medium heat, warm the olive oil and add the onion, carrots, and fennel. Cover and cook, stirring occasionally, until the vegetables are soft and caramel in color. Add the wine and squash and cover with the broth. Simmer, uncovered, for about 30 minutes, or until the squash is very soft.

Purée the soup in the pot with a handheld immersion blender, or purée in a food processor (working in batches) and return it to the pot. Add the thyme, coriander, and cinnamon, and season with salt and pepper to taste. Add the coconut or cashew milk, taste for sweetness, and add maple syrup to taste. Heat the soup and thin with extra broth if necessary.

To serve, ladle the soup into bowls and sprinkle with the dried figs and pine nuts.

KITCHEN TIP
To make cashew milk, purée 2 1/2 to 3 cups water with 1 cup cashews in a blender and strain in a fine-mesh strainer.

CREAMY CAULIFLOWER AND PASTA

6

SERVINGS

Cauliflower is a favorite of mine, and in this recipe, it takes the place of meat. I like cauliflower cooked all possible ways, but I am especially fond of it cooked as my mother did—until it is soft, creamy, and sweet.

1 head cauliflower, cut into florets

1 pound whole wheat pasta, such as shells or rotelle

⅓ cup extra-virgin olive oil

4 garlic cloves, thinly sliced

½ cup dry white wine

1½ tablespoons chopped fresh oregano

¼ cup kalamata olives, pitted and chopped

1 teaspoon red-pepper flakes

4 sprigs fresh Italian parsley, stemmed and chopped

Salt

Freshly ground black pepper

¼ cup shredded Asiago or Parmesan cheese (about 1 ounce)

Bring a large pot of salted water to a boil over high heat. Add the cauliflower and cook for 5 minutes, or until tender. Remove with a slotted spoon to a medium bowl, reserving the water. Cook the pasta according to package directions in the reserved water. Drain and transfer to a large serving bowl.

While the pasta is cooking, in a large skillet, heat the oil over medium-high heat. Add the garlic and cauliflower and cook for 5 minutes, stirring and breaking the cauliflower into bite-size pieces. Add the wine, oregano, olives, and red-pepper flakes and cook for 3 minutes, or until the cauliflower is very tender. Add the parsley and season with salt and pepper to taste. Pour over the pasta and toss to coat well. Top with the cheese.

VARIATION
For additional color, add a small can of drained and chopped tomatoes to the skillet when you add the wine.

SIMPLY ORGANIC

PENNE WITH BEETS, BEET GREENS, AND GOAT CHEESE

MAKES
6
SERVINGS

I have worked with Stanford University's education department to create a no-recipe, low-budget cooking class with minimal instructions for teachers to take back to their classrooms. They harvest whatever is growing in my garden, toss it with whole grain pasta, and add a little cheese. The result is a lesson plan that begins in the garden and ends in the kitchen. This dish was one they initially turned their noses up at, but they walked away saying it was one of the yummiest they had ever eaten.

2 bunches medium beets with greens (about 8 beets)

½ cup olive oil

1 medium onion, thinly sliced

2 garlic cloves

3 tablespoons balsamic vinegar

2 tablespoons chopped fresh oregano

2 tablespoons chopped fresh rosemary

1 pound whole wheat penne

Salt

Freshly ground black pepper

6 ounces soft goat cheese, such as chèvre

3 ounces Asiago or Parmesan cheese, grated

Cut the greens off the beets and set aside. Trim the tops and bottoms of the beets and put the beets in a large pot. Cover with water and bring to a simmer over medium-high heat. Cook for 20 minutes to 1 hour, depending upon the size of the beets. When the beets are cooked, remove and run under cold water, using your hands to slip off the skins. Cut the beets into bite-size wedges.

While the beets are cooking, wash the beet greens thoroughly and chop coarsely. Bring another large pot of water to a boil for the pasta.

In a large skillet, over medium heat, warm the olive oil and add the onion and garlic. Cook, stirring occasionally, for 5 minutes or until soft.

Add the vinegar, oregano, and rosemary and cook for 1 minute, stirring to break up the brown bits.

Cook the penne according to the package directions, adding the beet greens during the last 1 minute of cooking. Drain, reserving ½ cup of the cooking water, and return the pasta to the pot.

Add the beets and onion mixture to the pot with pasta, tossing gently to mix. Season with salt and pepper to taste.

On a large platter, dollop the goat cheese randomly across the surface. Sprinkle with half the grated cheese. Spoon a few tablespoons of the pasta water over the cheeses to warm them and make them saucy. Spoon the pasta on top and serve immediately.

POLENTA WITH THREE CHEESES AND MARINARA

When I was a kid, my Nana made polenta a lot. She frequently served it with a creamy salt cod dish called *baccalà,* but my brothers and I hated it (now I would kill for a bowl of her *baccalà*). So Nana topped the polenta with marinara, mozzarella, provolone, and grated Parmesan. It's real kids' food.

1½ cups coarsely ground polenta

½ teaspoon salt

½ cup shredded smoked mozzarella cheese (about 4 ounces)

½ cup shredded provolone cheese (about 4 ounces)

⅓ cup grated Parmesan, Asiago, or Romano cheese (about 1½ ounces)

2 cups pasta sauce, heated

2 tablespoons chopped fresh oregano

2 tablespoons chopped fresh Italian parsley

In a medium saucepan over medium heat, bring 5 cups water to a boil. Gradually add the polenta and salt, stirring constantly. Cook, stirring often, for 30 minutes, or until the polenta thickens and is creamy. Add the mozzarella and provolone, stirring until the cheeses are melted and well blended. Stir in ¼ cup of the Parmesan cheese.

Divide the polenta evenly among 6 shallow bowls. Top with the pasta sauce and sprinkle with the oregano, parsley, and the remaining Parmesan.

KITCHEN TIP

Be sure to watch the polenta and add more water if it seems to dry out too quickly. My grandmother used to cook polenta for hours, adding water when needed. Her polenta was the smoothest and most delicious I have ever eaten. Although we don't have the time that our grandmothers did to spend in the kitchen, be sure that your polenta is cooked to the consistency of porridge.

CHICKEN-VEGETABLE SOUP WITH NOODLES

In the winter, the aroma of chicken soup simmering on the stove is as soothing as it gets. I love noodles in my soup, but 1½ cups cooked rice would work just as well for a change of pace.

1 whole chicken (3 to 4 pounds), cut up

2 large onions

3 large carrots, chopped

2 celery ribs, chopped

5 peppercorns

2 large sprigs fresh dill

3 large sprigs fresh Italian parsley

1 parsnip, chopped

1 teaspoon salt

½ teaspoon freshly ground black pepper

12 ounces wide or thin egg noodles

Put the chicken, 1 onion, 1 carrot, 1 celery rib, the peppercorns, dill, and parsley in a large stockpot. Cover with cold water. Bring to a boil over high heat. Reduce the heat to low, cover, and simmer for 4 hours. Cool slightly.

Place a sieve over a large bowl and strain the broth. Set aside the chicken and discard all the remaining solids. Refrigerate the broth for at least 3 hours or overnight, until congealed and the fat has risen to the top.

Meanwhile, remove the chicken from the bones and shred into bite-size pieces. Discard the chicken skin and bones and refrigerate the meat.

When the broth is completely chilled, remove and discard the fat from the top of the broth. Chop the remaining onion, 2 carrots, and celery rib.

In a large stockpot, combine the broth, the chopped vegetables, parsnip, salt, and black pepper. Bring to a boil over high heat. Reduce the heat to low, cover, and simmer for 1 hour.

Meanwhile, bring a large pot of water to a boil and cook the noodles according to the package directions.

Add the noodles and chicken to the broth and simmer for 5 minutes, or until heated through.

KITCHEN TIPS

Chicken soup may be prepared many ways. Sometimes I like to keep the noodles separate from the broth, putting the cooked noodles into soup bowls and topping with the broth. If I don't want to use another pot, I will cook the noodles in the broth. This will thicken and cloud the soup a bit, but it is another delicious way to eat this classic dish.

If I am in a hurry but want some home-made soup, I will use boneless, skinless chicken breasts and prepared chicken broth, and simmer them for about an hour with the seasonings and vegetables.

CHICKEN WITH DRIED CHERRIES, CAPERS, AND CHILES

The combination of the richly sweet cherries, salty capers, and spicy chiles may seem odd at first, but after one bite, you will want to make this often because the flavors are so marvelous. I prefer using chicken breasts on the bone, as they are much juicier. If you are in a crunch for time, however, use boneless ones and reduce the roasting time to 25 minutes.

1 teaspoon paprika

¼ teaspoon salt

¼ teaspoon freshly ground black pepper

4 bone-in chicken breast halves, skinned

2 tablespoons extra-virgin olive oil

1 small red onion, chopped

1½ cups chicken broth

½ cup dried cherries

2 tablespoons capers

2 tablespoons honey

1 teaspoon ground cumin

1 cinnamon stick, broken in half

1 to 2 hot chile peppers, such as cayenne, red jalapeño, or habanero, seeded and minced

Preheat the oven to 400°F.

In a small bowl, combine the paprika, salt, and black pepper. Place the chicken in a large, shallow roasting pan. Brush with 1 tablespoon of the oil and sprinkle with the paprika mixture.

Roast for 45 minutes, or until a thermometer inserted in the thickest portion registers 180°F and the juices run clear.

Meanwhile, heat the remaining 1 tablespoon oil in a medium saucepan over medium heat. Cook the onion for 5 minutes, or until soft. Add the broth, cherries, capers, honey, cumin, and cinnamon stick. Bring to a boil, reduce the heat to medium-low, and simmer for 20 minutes, or until the cherries are plump and the sauce has thickened. Stir in the chile peppers.

When the chicken is cooked, for extra flavor, if desired, drain off the pan juices and stir them into the cherry sauce. Remove and discard the cinnamon stick before serving.

Place the chicken on a serving platter and top with the sauce.

PORK SHOULDER WITH CHIPOTLE-ORANGE BARBECUE SAUCE

MAKES
8
SERVINGS

Organic pork raised on small farms is easier to find these days. Heritage breeds of pig as well as lamb are more available, too. The flavor of these animals, when well raised, can be more distinctive than their confined, mass-produced counterparts. Serve this pork dish with your favorite coleslaw and squares of warm cornbread.

½ cup fresh orange juice

¼ cup honey

2 tablespoons red wine vinegar

2 tablespoons Dijon mustard

1 whole canned chipotle chile pepper, puréed or minced

1 tablespoon vegetable or light olive oil

2 garlic cloves, minced

1 tablespoon salt

1½ teaspoons ground cumin

½ teaspoon ground cinnamon

1 pork shoulder or butt roast (4 to 5 pounds)

2 tablespoons finely sliced green onions

Preheat the oven to 450°F.

In a small bowl, combine the orange juice, honey, vinegar, mustard, chile pepper, oil, garlic, salt, cumin, and cinnamon.

Put the pork in a roasting pan that can easily be covered and coat the pork completely with the sauce. Cover with a lid or foil.

Reduce oven temperature to 200°F. Roast the pork, without opening the door, for 5 hours.

Check to see if it is falling-apart tender, and if not, cover and roast for about 30 minutes longer, or until it is tender. Sprinkle green onions as a garnish.

KITCHEN TIP
This is a great slow-cooker dish. Just put everything in the pot and cook for 24 hours on low.

ZINFANDEL-BRAISED LAMB SHANKS

Braised meat is a perfect dish to prepare for dinner guests. These lamb shanks can be cooked hours in advance and kept warm in a low-heat oven. Or, prepare them the day before and reheat before serving; they will be even more flavorful this way. Serve on a bed of warm polenta or mashed potatoes.

4 lamb shanks (about 3 pounds), cut across the bone by your butcher into 3-inch slices

½ teaspoon salt

½ teaspoon freshly ground black pepper

1 bottle (750 ml) hearty Zinfandel

4 carrots, cut into 1-inch pieces

1 large onion, sliced

1 whole head of garlic, cut into thick slices

1 teaspoon whole mustard seeds

5 whole juniper berries (optional)

3 tablespoons unsalted butter

¼ cup chopped fresh rosemary

Preheat the oven to 500°F. Put the lamb in a heavy roasting pan and sprinkle with ¼ teaspoon of the salt and ¼ teaspoon of the pepper. Roast for 30 minutes, or until browned, turning once.

Reduce the oven temperature to 350°F. Add the Zinfandel, carrots, onion, garlic, mustard seeds, and juniper berries, if using. Roast for 2 hours, or until the lamb is very tender and nearly falling off the bone, turning the shanks and basting with the sauce every 20 minutes. Remove the lamb, carrots, and garlic to a large platter. Keep warm.

Strain the sauce through a cheesecloth-lined sieve into a small saucepan. Bring to a boil over high heat. Cook for 5 minutes, or until reduced by half. If the sauce seems too thin, lower the heat to medium and reduce it to the desired thickness. Whisk in the butter. Add the remaining ¼ teaspoon salt and ¼ teaspoon pepper, or season to taste. Pour the sauce over the meat and carrots and sprinkle with the rosemary.

SAFFRON COUSCOUS

In this couscous dish, the aroma of the saffron blends beautifully with the raisins, especially when all three are finished with a drizzle of pan juices from whatever meat you might be cooking for dinner. It goes well with roasted leg of lamb or chicken.

2 cups vegetable or chicken broth

½ cup raisins

2 tablespoons unsalted butter

½ teaspoon salt

¼ teaspoon saffron threads, crumbled

2 cups couscous

½ cup pine nuts

4 green onions, thinly sliced

In a medium saucepan over high heat, bring the broth to a boil. Add the raisins, butter, salt, and saffron, stirring until the butter melts. Remove from the heat and stir in the couscous. Cover tightly and set aside for 5 minutes.

Meanwhile, put the pine nuts in a small, heavy-bottomed skillet over medium heat. Cook, shaking the skillet often, for 5 minutes, or until lightly browned and toasted.

Fluff the couscous and stir in the pine nuts and green onions.

LENTILS, FENNEL, AND OLIVES

Served warm or at room temperature, this simple lentil dish is delicious as a first course or side dish with lamb or chicken.

2 cups cooked lentils (see Kitchen Tip)

½ cup olive oil

½ small red onion, thinly sliced

1 cup thinly sliced fennel

1 garlic clove, finely chopped

2 to 3 tablespoons fresh lemon juice

½ cup chopped pitted olives, such as kalamata or another flavorful olive

2 to 3 tablespoons chopped fresh chervil

⅓ cup chopped fresh Italian parsley

Salt

Freshly ground black pepper

½ cup crumbled feta cheese

In a medium bowl, combine the lentils, oil, onion, fennel, garlic, lemon juice, olives, chervil, and ¼ cup of the parsley. Allow to sit at room temperature for 30 minutes. Toss and season with salt and pepper.

Transfer the lentil mixture to a serving plate and sprinkle with feta and the remaining parsley.

KITCHEN TIP

Darker lentils, such as brown and green, take more time to cook than orange, red, or yellow lentils. The darker colors also do not disintegrate as quickly as the brighter ones. To cook lentils: Put the lentils in a pan, add enough water to cover by about 2 inches, and bring to a boil. Cook for 2 minutes, lower the heat, and simmer for 10 minutes to 1 hour, depending upon the type of lentil. Taste for doneness.

PARSLEY ROOT GRATIN
WITH GRUYÈRE CHEESE

There are a handful of dishes that I make over and over again because people always go back for seconds. This is one of those unbeatable dishes: layers of thinly sliced vegetables, scented with onions and fennel and bound together with a creamy sauce.

1 large parsley root (about 1 pound), peeled and thinly sliced (see Kitchen Tips)

2 russet potatoes, peeled and thinly sliced

2 medium fennel bulbs, thinly sliced

½ cup unbleached all-purpose flour

½ teaspoon salt

½ teaspoon freshly ground black pepper

4 cups milk

3 cups shredded Gruyère or Swiss cheese (about 12 ounces)

Preheat the oven to 350°F. Lightly butter a 3-quart baking dish.

Put the parsley root, potatoes, and fennel in a large bowl and toss well.

In a medium bowl, combine the flour, salt, and pepper. Whisk in the milk.

Layer one-third of the vegetables in the prepared baking dish. Sprinkle with one-third of the cheese. Repeat the layers once more. Add the remaining third of the vegetables, but don't add the rest of the cheese yet. Pour the milk mixture over all, pressing the vegetables so they are moistened by the milk. Sprinkle the remaining third of the cheese on top.

Bake for 1 hour, or until the vegetables are very tender. Serve immediately.

KITCHEN TIPS

If you can't find parsley root, substitute celery root.

For a low-fat version, increase the flour to ¾ cup and use vegetable broth or low-fat milk. For a luscious, decadent version, substitute half-and-half or heavy cream for the milk and omit the flour.

MARINATED MUSHROOMS WITH LEMON AND OREGANO

I always find it intriguing to take common ingredients, such as domestic button mushrooms (especially now that you can find them organically grown), and transform them into something wonderful and simple, like this recipe.

¼ cup extra-virgin olive oil

2 tablespoons fresh lemon juice

2 green onions, minced

2 garlic cloves, minced

1½ tablespoons chopped fresh savory, or 1½ teaspoons dried savory or marjoram

2 to 3 tablespoons chopped fresh Italian parsley

1 pound button mushrooms, stemmed and thinly sliced

Salt

Freshly ground black pepper

1 head butter lettuce, leaves separated

In a medium bowl, combine the oil, lemon juice, green onions, garlic, savory, and parsley. Cover and refrigerate for at least 1 hour.

About 30 minutes before serving, add the mushrooms to the bowl and toss to coat well. Season with salt and pepper to taste. Allow to stand at room temperature for 15 minutes.

Arrange the lettuce leaves on a large serving platter or on 6 individual salad plates. Mound the mushrooms in the center.

KITCHEN TIP
For a lovely simple lunch, add 1 pound roasted chicken or seasoned tofu to the mushrooms before serving.

JICAMA, RADISH, AND AVOCADO SALAD

The complex, fresh flavors of this crunchy salad are the perfect accompaniment to a bowl of hot soup served with fresh bread.

2 avocados, halved, peeled, pitted, and chopped

1 pound jicama, peeled and cut into matchsticks

12 radishes, very thinly sliced

3 tablespoons olive oil

3 tablespoons red wine vinegar

Juice of 1 lime

2 tablespoons chopped fresh chives

1 tablespoon sugar

½ teaspoon salt

Pinch of red-pepper flakes (optional)

In a medium bowl, combine the avocados, jicama, radishes, oil, vinegar, lime juice, chives, sugar, salt, and red-pepper flakes, if using; toss to coat well.

ROSEMARY-LEMON BISCUITS

There are a handful of standard recipes that I have taught my children, so that no matter where or in what situation, they can create from scratch something that will make people happy. I have yet to meet anyone who doesn't like warm biscuits. These drop biscuits are the easiest to prepare, with no need for kneading or rolling the dough. My sons make them often.

1 cup buttermilk (see Organic Tip on page 38)

1 large egg, beaten

1 tablespoon grated lemon zest

2 teaspoons finely chopped fresh rosemary

2 cups whole grain pastry flour

1 tablespoon baking powder

1 teaspoon salt

½ cup (1 stick) cold unsalted butter

Preheat the oven to 375°F. Line a baking sheet with parchment paper.

In a small bowl, combine the buttermilk, egg, lemon zest, and rosemary.

In a medium bowl, combine the flour, baking powder, and salt. Grate the butter into the mixture. Using your hands or a pastry blender, work the butter into the flour mixture until the pieces are about the size of peas. Form a well in the center of the flour mixture and stir in the buttermilk mixture just until blended.

Drop the batter by heaping tablespoons onto the prepared baking sheet to form 12 biscuits. Bake for 12 to 15 minutes, or until golden and a wooden pick inserted in the center of a biscuit comes out clean.

STEAMED VANILLA CUSTARD WITH BANANAS

Forget about turning on the oven or dirtying a pot, and throw away that box of instant pudding. This delicate, moist custard can be prepared in thirty minutes. It is the kind of dessert that I sneak out of bed for and eat as a midnight snack by the light of the refrigerator. You will need a steamer insert that is large enough to hold six ramekins.

2 large eggs

1 cup whole milk

½ cup sugar

1 teaspoon vanilla extract

2 bananas, sliced

Sprinkle of ground cinnamon

Fill a large pot with 2 inches of water. Bring to a boil over high heat.

Meanwhile, in a medium bowl, whisk the eggs with the milk. Whisk in the sugar and vanilla extract.

Divide the bananas evenly among six 8-ounce heatproof bowls or ramekins. Pour the custard evenly over the bananas. Sprinkle lightly with cinnamon. Cover each bowl with foil. Place the bowls in a large steamer insert that fits into the pot with the boiling water. Remove the pot of boiling water from the heat and put the steamer insert into the pot. Return the pot to the heat and return the water to a boil. Reduce the heat to low, cover, and simmer for 25 minutes, or until a knife inserted in the center of the custard comes out clean.

CHOCOLATE MERINGUES WITH FRUIT SAUCE

MAKES
6
SERVINGS

This beautiful dessert is a low-fat version of a fruit tart. I call for apricots, but use whatever dried fruit you would like. Dried apples, pears, or peaches work nicely. Or, why not use a mixture of several dried fruits? Make these meringues on a crisp, dry day.

½ cup confectioners' sugar

2 tablespoons unsweetened cocoa powder

¼ teaspoon ground cinnamon

2 large egg whites, at room temperature

¼ cup whole almonds or hazelnuts

1½ cups orange juice

1 tablespoon honey

⅛ teaspoon freshly grated nutmeg

12 large dried apricot halves, thinly sliced

Preheat the oven to 200°F. Line a large baking sheet with parchment paper.

In a small bowl, combine the confectioners' sugar, cocoa, and cinnamon.

Put the egg whites in a large bowl and, using an electric mixer on high speed, beat until soft peaks form. Reduce the speed to low and gradually add the sugar mixture, one-third at a time, beating for 3 minutes between additions, until stiff, glossy peaks form.

Spoon the mixture onto the prepared baking sheet, forming 6 ovals about 3 inches thick. Bake for 2 hours. If the meringues are still not dry, turn off the oven and leave them in the oven for 1 hour. Cool on the baking sheet on a rack.

Meanwhile, put the nuts in a small skillet over medium heat. Cook, shaking the skillet often, for 5 minutes, or until lightly browned and toasted. Set aside to cool slightly. Chop the nuts.

Add the orange juice, honey, nutmeg, and apricots to the skillet. Bring to a boil over medium-high heat. Reduce the heat to low and simmer for 20 minutes, or until the apricots plump and the sauce reduces and thickens slightly.

To serve, spoon a generous amount of the apricot sauce onto 6 plates. Place a meringue on top of each and drizzle the remaining sauce over the meringues. Sprinkle with the nuts.

OAT BERRY CUSTARD
WITH DRIED CHERRIES

I love this nutty custard for breakfast or dessert. In winter, using dried fruit instead of out-of-season fresh is a good way to make use of organic seasonal ingredients.

1 cup oat berries (groats)
½ **teaspoon salt**
⅓ **cup dried cherries**
¼ **cup maple syrup**
2 large eggs

1 cup milk
⅓ **cup sugar**
½ **teaspoon vanilla extract**
Sprinkling of ground cinnamon

In a medium saucepan over medium heat, bring 4 cups water to a boil. Add the oat berries and salt. Reduce the heat to low, cover, and simmer, stirring occasionally, for 35 minutes, or until the liquid is absorbed. Remove from the heat and add the cherries and maple syrup. Keep covered and set aside to cool to room temperature.

Preheat the oven to 350°F. Place four 10-ounce ovenproof bowls or ramekins in a large, shallow baking dish.

In a medium bowl, whisk the eggs until light and creamy. Whisk in the milk, sugar, and vanilla extract.

Divide the oatmeal equally among the prepared bowls or ramekins. Pour the custard evenly on top of each. Sprinkle each lightly with cinnamon. Pour enough cold water into the baking dish to come about 1½ inches up the sides of the bowls.

Bake the custard for 30 to 40 minutes, or until a knife inserted in the center comes out clean.

KITCHEN TIP
Instead of cherries, use any dried fruit about the same size, such as raisins or cranberries, or cut-up pieces of dried apricots, dates, pears, figs, or prunes.

LUNDBERG FAMILY FARMS

For as long as I can remember, the only rice we have used in our restaurants is Lundberg, which is organically grown in California. The many rices from the Lundbergs' family-operated farms are unfailingly delicious and of the highest quality. Their old-fashioned, earnest efforts at farming organically with environmental consciousness have remained unchanged over the years.

The company traces its roots back to 1937, when Albert and Frances Lundberg left western Nebraska with their four sons, Eldon, Wendell, Harlan, and Homer. During the Dust Bowl years, Albert saw huge tracts of land across the Midwest erode. Nutrient-giving organic matter had disappeared from the soil, and fierce winds created enormous dust clouds that made life miserable and farming impossible. Albert decided to move his family to Richvale, to begin a new life of farming in Northern California. The Sacramento Valley was the perfect setting for Albert Lundberg to pass on his legacy to his four sons.

The four Lundberg brothers were deeply influenced by their father. They believed in ecological farming long before it was fashionable. Influenced by the Dust Bowl, which was such an ecological and agricultural catastrophe, they have developed a special relationship with nature. For almost seventy years, Lundberg Family Farms has been using methods of farming that are beneficial for the soil, wildlife, air, and water.

"We believe healthy soil will produce healthy food. We believe the soil is a living thing, and as such, needs to be fed and cared for," says Harlan Lundberg.

This special concern for the environment is equaled only by the company's concern for product quality. Today, Lundberg Family Farms specializes in farming organic brown rice and manufactures over 150 rice products, including wild rice and multigrain pilafs. They work hard to provide consumers with rice and rice products of superior quality, wholesomeness, and flavor. And it shows in their products.

ORGANIC RESOURCES

Here's a list of companies offering organic products. It is just a sampling of all the products available, but will give you a good starting point. The company Web sites offer information about organic food and an organic lifestyle.

GROCERY PRODUCTS

AH! LASKA

Chocolate syrup and cocoa
www.ahlaska.com

Alvarado St. Bakery

Whole grain breads and bagels
www.alvaradostreetbakery.com

Arrowhead Mills

Whole grain cereals, beans, flours, baking mixes, and nut butters
www.arrowheadmills.com

Baby's Only Organic

Baby formula and juices
www.naturesone.com

Barbara's Bakery

Cereals, cookies, crackers, and snack bars
www.barbarasbakery.com

Bearitos

Chips and snacks
www.bearitos.com

Bob's Red Mill

Flours, whole grains, beans, seeds, and spices
www.bobsredmill.com

Cascadian Farm

Frozen fruits, fruit juices, and vegetables; fruit spreads, granola bars, and cereal
www.cascadianfarm.com

Diamond Organics

Organic produce, meats, pastries, breads, and complete meals; gift baskets, wine, and flowers, all shipped to your doorstep
www.diamondorganics.com

Earth's Best Organic

Baby food, cereals, formula, and juices
www.earthsbest.com

Eden Foods

Canned beans and vegetables; whole grains, pastas, oils, and vinegars; soy products; condiments and sweeteners; Asian products and snack foods
www.edenfoods.com

Fantastic Foods

Grains and soup mixes
www.fantasticfoods.com

Florida Crystals

Sugars, syrups, and rice
www.floridacrystals.com

French Meadow Bakery

Whole grain breads, bagels, tortillas, and pizza crusts
www.frenchmeadow.com

Frontier Natural Products Co-op

Dried herbs, spices, seasonings; dried foods; teas; dips and dressing mixes
www.frontierherb.com

Good Sense

Dried fruits, nuts, and trail mixes
www.waymouthfarms.com

Happy Baby

Frozen baby meals
www.happybabyfood.com

Horizon Organic Dairy

Milk, cheese, sour cream, yogurt, fruit juices
www.horizonorganic.com

Imagine Foods

Prepared soups, broths, and stocks
www.imaginefoods.com

R.W. Knudsen

Juices
www.knudsenjuices.com

Lundberg Family Farms

Rice and specialty rice products
www.lundberg.com

MaraNatha

Nut butters
www.maranathanutbutters.com

Muir Glen Organic

Canned and jarred tomato products
www.muirglen.com

Natural Choice

Frozen fruits and vegetables; sorbets and ice cream
www.ncf-inc.com

Nature's Path

Breakfast cereals, cereal bars, breads, and waffles; baking mixes, pasta, and snack foods
www.naturespath.com

Newman's Own Organics

Snack foods, including cookies
www.newmansownorganics.com

The Organic Cow of Vermont

Dairy products
www.theorganiccow.com

Organic Valley

Dairy products and soy milk; fruit juices, eggs, and meats
www.organicvalley.com

Pacific Natural Foods

Soups, broths, sauces, and gravies; nut and grain beverages
www.pacificfoods.com

Pavich Family Farms

Raisins, prunes, and dates
www.pavich.com

Rapunzel Pure Organics

Baking chocolate, whole cane sugar, Swiss chocolate bars, coffees, cocoa drink mixes, and soup broths
www.rapunzel.com

Rudi's Organic Bakery

Whole grain breads, rolls, English muffins, and tortillas
www.rudisbakery.com

Seeds of Change

Salad dressings, sauces, salsa, and prepared meals
www.seedsofchangefoods.com

ShariAnn's Organic

Canned soups, beans, and pumpkin
www.shariannsorganic.com

Spectrum Organics

Cooking oils
www.spectrumorganics.com

Stonyfield Farm

Milk, dairy and soy yogurt
www.stonyfield.com

Sunspire

Cookie bars, candies, and baking chips
www.sunspire.com

MEATS AND POULTRY

Completely organic meats and poultry are still very hard to find. Here's a list of companies that are producing some products that are either organic or as close to organic as possible.

Applegate Farms

Deli meats and cheeses, bacon, burgers, and hot dogs
www.applegatefarms.com

Coleman Natural

Beef, pork, chicken, and sausage
www.colemannatural.com

Damar Farms Organic Red Angus Meats

Beef shipped to your home
www.damarfarms.com

Davis Mountains

Beef shipped to your home
www.davismountainorganicbeef.com

Jamison Farm

Lamb and lamb products
www.jamisonfarm.com

Niman Ranch

Beef, pork, and lamb
www.nimanranch.com

Organic Prairie Family of Farms

Beef, pork, chicken, and turkey
www.organicprairie.com

Sommers Organic

Beef, pork, chicken, and other poultry, sold
fresh and frozen
www.sommersorganic.com

Wholesome Harvest Organic Meats

Beef, pork, lamb, chicken, and turkey shipped
to your home
www.wholesomeharvest.com

FRESH PRODUCE

Cal-Organic Farms

Fresh fruits and vegetables
www.calorganicfarms.com

Driscoll's

Berries
www.driscolls.com

Earthbound Farm

Fresh vegetables and fruits, including
precut snack packs; dried fruit, snacks,
and packaged juices
www.ebfarm.com

Frieda's

Fruits and vegetables
www.friedas.com

Grateful Harvest

Organic packaged produce
www.gratefulharvest.com

Stemilt

Fruits
www.stemilt.com

BEERS AND WINES

I have only included producers in the United States,
though there are many European organic wines and
beers available.

Amity ECO-WINE

Oregon reds and whites
www.amityvineyards.com

Bonterra

California reds and whites
www.bonterra.com

Butte Creek Brewery

Ale, porter, and pilsner
www.buttecreek.com

Chateau Lorane

Oregon reds and whites
www.chateaulorane.com

Cooper Mountain Vineyards

Oregon reds and whites
www.coopermountainwine.com

Frey Winery

California reds and whites
www.freywine.com

Frog's Leap

California reds and whites
www.frogsleap.com

LaRocca Vineyards

California reds, whites, and blush
www.laroccavineyards.com

Lolonis

California reds and whites
www.lolonis.com

Maysara Estate Winery

Oregon reds and whites
www.maysara.com

Natureland

Ale and lager
www.pwbrewing.com

Organic Wine Works

Organic reds and whites
www.organicwineworks.com

Orleans Hill

California reds and whites
www.ourdailyred.com

Peak Organic

Organic beer
www.peakbrewing.com

Wolaver's Organic Ales & Hard Cider

Ales and hard cider
www.wolavers.com
www.ottercreekbrewing.com

ORGANIC INFORMATION

Acres USA
www.acresusa.com

All Organic Links
www.allorganiclinks.com

Biodynamics
www.biodynamics.com

California Certified Organic Farmers
www.ccof.org

CSA Farms
www.csafarms.org

Eat Well Guide
www.eatwellguide.org

Food & Water Watch
www.foodandwaterwatch.com

The Green Guide
www.thegreenguide.com

Green People
www.greenpeople.org

Local Harvest
www.localharvest.org

Organic Alliance
www.organic.org

Organic Authority
www.organicauthority.com

Organic Consumers Association
www.organicconsumers.org

Organic Kitchen
www.organickitchen.com

Organic Trade Association
www.ota.com
www.theorganicpages.com

Monterey Bay Aquarium Seafood Watch Program
www.montereybayaquarium.org/cr/
seafoodwatch.asp

Mothers & Others
www.mothers.org

Rodale Institute
www.rodaleinstitute.org

Sustainable Food News
www.sustainablefoodnews.com

Sustainable News Center
www.sustainablenews.org

Sustainable Table
www.sustainabletable.org

USDA National Organics Program
www.ams.usda.gov/nop

INDEX

TABLE OF EQUIVALENTS

The exact equivalents in the following tables have been rounded for convenience.

Liquid/Dry Measurements

U.S.	Metric
¼ teaspoon	1.25 milliliters
½ teaspoon	2.5 milliliters
1 teaspoon	5 milliliters
1 tablespoon (3 teaspoons)	15 milliliters
1 fluid ounce (2 tablespoons)	30 milliliters
¼ cup	60 milliliters
⅓ cup	80 milliliters
½ cup	120 milliliters
1 cup	240 milliliters
1 pint (2 cups)	480 milliliters
1 quart (4 cups, 32 ounces)	960 milliliters
1 gallon (4 quarts)	3.84 liters
1 ounce (by weight)	28 grams
1 pound	448 grams
2.2 pounds	1 kilogram

Lengths

U.S.	Metric
⅛ inch	3 millimeters
¼ inch	6 millimeters
½ inch	12 millimeters
1 inch	2.5 centimeters

Oven Temperature

Fahrenheit	Celsius	Gas
250	120	½
275	140	1
300	150	2
325	160	3
350	180	4
375	190	5
400	200	6
425	220	7
450	230	8
475	240	9
500	260	10